Festival of the Flame

London 2012
Paralympic Games
Closing Ceremony
9 September 2012

Please note, the Ceremony includes strobe lighting, pyrotechnics and lasers.

HRH The Earl of Wessex

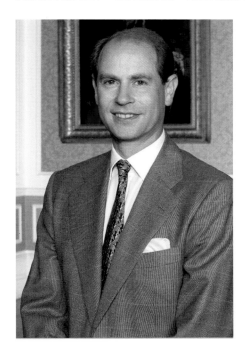

The Closing Ceremony of the London 2012 Paralympic Games gives us a chance to reflect on a most extraordinary festival of sport and celebration.

This evening we particularly recognise the endeavours and achievements of Paralympians. Once again they've shown a spirit of sportsmanship which frankly leaves most of us feeling pretty humble yet at the same time uplifted. We all owe the International Paralympic Committee and all the Paralympic sports federations a huge debt of gratitude for entrusting London with the Games and helping to deliver such a spectacular festival of sport.

Any event on this scale requires a huge effort both to organise and to run. This evening is a very poignant moment for the London 2012 Organising Committee, the venue managers and staff, as well as the countless volunteers who have worked so hard to deliver the Games since the bid was won in 2005. While some of us celebrate a huge success and enjoy the festivities, there will be others for whom this event will evoke very strong and mixed emotions of joy, relief and not a little sadness as new-found friends disperse to their homes.

Ten years ago, The Queen's Golden Jubilee year, the Commonwealth gathered in Manchester for the XVIIth Commonwealth Games. So it seems particularly fitting that for Her Majesty's Diamond Jubilee the world should have descended on London to help us celebrate an extraordinary year in the history of this kingdom, the birthplace of the Paralympic Movement, and once again that sport should have been the catalyst.

Thank you everyone for helping to make 2012 such a very special year, especially for our Queen.

Sebastian Coe

Chair, London 2012 Organising Committee

After seven years of planning and preparations involving the whole city, country and most of the world, our time and our responsibilities as hosts of the Olympic and Paralympic Games have almost come to an end.

As we join the world for a grand global goodbye to the Paralympic athletes, teams and sports officials at this evening's Closing Ceremony, I would like to thank everyone who has been a part of this historic odyssey of human achievement and endeavour.

We journeyed to the British 'Isles of Wonder' and to a 'Green and Pleasant Land', where we staged the Olympic Games for an historic third occasion in London, and we welcomed the Paralympic Movement back to its spiritual home and birthplace, a movement that was reborn 64 years after Stoke Mandeville as the world's second-biggest sporting event.

We also journeyed to 'Enlightenment' and 'A Brave New World' where we saw 'Spirit in Motion'. We were moved, dazzled and inspired by Paralympic athletes who refused to say no, and provided sporting performances of stunning imagination, creativity, courage and determination.

The Paralympic athletes showed what is possible – that sport is about what you can do, what you can overcome, the barriers and attitudes you can break, that the human spirit is stronger than steel and far more resilient than many thought possible.

Most importantly, this was a journey of inspiration for everyone, especially young people, and I would like to thank the millions of people across the country and around the world, people of all ages and from all cultures and backgrounds – from scientists and Shakespearean actors, to teachers, nurses, bus drivers, the men and women in uniform, and especially our much-admired Games Maker volunteers, coaches, parents and sports club volunteers and many, many others from all walks of life and levels of ability who made this journey possible for us and the athletes.

You have made these Games a triumph of human endeavour and international collaboration and helped make a statement about why sport matters so much as a catalyst for hope and change in difficult and challenging times. You have inspired a generation and made London 2012 a very special time in the lives of people everywhere.

Rt Hon David Cameron MP

Prime Minister

The close of these fantastic Paralympic Games marks the close of London 2012, but not the end of the great things these Games will achieve.

The past few days have not only shown us some outstanding performances and created new role models, but mark a major step forward in the status of Paralympic sport. A Movement that began in Britain over six decades ago has become one of the largest international sporting events on the planet, attracting crowds and gripping viewers on television.

The inspirational power of Paralympic athletes has shown us what can be achieved, and proved that records are there to be broken. Rather than be constrained by what some see as limits, these athletes have excelled, and in doing so helped change attitudes to disability forever.

I am delighted with that success, and the positive impact on society, just as I have been thrilled by the quality of the sport we have all seen. This has been a summer of brilliant achievements that will never be forgotten – and lives will be transformed as a result.

Sir Philip Craven

President of the International Paralympic Committee

'Every chance that you get is a chance you seize'.

As we gather for the Closing Ceremony, I believe this lyric from Coldplay's 'Speed of Sound' can act as a motto for everyone involved in making the London 2012 Paralympic Games a truly fantastic showcase of sport and the power of the human spirit.

All parties involved in these Games, including LOCOG, athletes, Games officials, volunteers, staff members and the great city of London, have grasped the opportunity to put on a global spectacle that will be remembered forever.

Tonight is a celebration, marking the achievements of everyone who has made these Games a tremendous success. On 29 August we opened with the theme of 'Enlightenment'. Tonight we are enlightened and armed with a superior knowledge of what can be achieved by all.

The legacy of these Games will be long-lasting. You only have to consider the impact the 1948 Stoke Mandeville Games had on the global sporting landscape to imagine what effect these Games will have in the coming months, years and decades.

For all athletes competing here on the world stage, in front of billions, these Games have been the opportunity of a lifetime. Their performances have delivered something far more tangible than medals. They have ensured that the world is a more equitable place than it was 12 days ago.

All can be rightly proud of their achievements. They have preserved the vision Sir Ludwig Guttmann had 64 years ago and taken it to a whole new level.

Boris Johnson

Mayor of London

Tonight the curtain falls on London's magical summer. As I pass the Paralympic Flag to Mayor Paes of Rio de Janeiro, and with it London's best wishes for the people of Brazil and their Games in four years' time, it is worth reflecting on what that Flag leaves behind.

Britain has always cherished its Paralympic heritage, from the birth of the Movement on these shores 64 years ago to the outstanding performances of our Paralympic team at recent Games. But this year, our capital has finally earned the title of Paralympic Host City, and no Londoner is more proud of that than me.

Because London's Paralympic legacy amounts to more than just memories. Part of the inheritance is plain to see, in bricks and mortar: this Stadium, our other venues and the Olympic Park itself have set new standards for accessibility

and inclusion. It can even be seen in the medieval cobblestones of London's historic South Bank walkway, which has enjoyed its own Paralympic-inspired makeover and is now easier to negotiate than ever before. And not forgetting where it all started, we've given a boost to grassroots disability sport as part of our sport legacy plan.

We are not complacent: despite our achievements, there are more barriers to overcome before life in London is as inclusive and accessible as we would like it to be. Inspired by the Paralympic Games, we embark on the next stage of that journey today with a determination that would make any Paralympian proud.

WELCOME

Kim Gavin

**Artistic Director, London 2012
Paralympic Games Closing Ceremony**

Welcome to the Closing Ceremony of the London 2012
Paralympic Games.

In a nation famous for festivals, this evening's 'Festival
of the Flame' is a celebration of the ancient and modern
traditions that have gathered down the ages, drawing on
the ever-changing seasons that define us – from autumn
equinox to summer solstice.

I couldn't be more delighted that Coldplay – one of
the world's bestselling music acts – will be leading the
celebrations. They'll perform a live and one-off concert,
and you'll hear some of their most iconic music, from 'Us
Against the World' and 'Yellow' to 'Clocks' and 'Viva La Vida',
alongside a cast of nearly 2,000 and some special guests.

For the 4,200 athletes who trained tirelessly to get here,
the Games are over and it's time to celebrate. We'll be
paying tribute to their endeavours and achievements
over the past 11 days, and saluting the 70,000 volunteers
who've helped to make it all possible, before finally
extinguishing the Flame that's burned so brightly in
London and will ignite again in Rio, four years from now.

And as we approach the dizzying climax of our
gathering, we will do so with a smile, knowing we were
entranced and enchanted by kindred spirits, fellow
keepers of the Flame and proud Paralympians.

Last one to leave the Stadium… please turn off the lights.

DREAMERS

The scene is serene and dreamy.

After 11 days of toil and exertion, the Paralympians are at rest.

They're joined by a tribe of weary Dreamers at the ancient site of Agitos, where they've come to raise three crescent moons from the earth. To achieve the seemingly impossible requires spirit and passion beyond the normal self. So we look towards the Dreamers to help us achieve our goals and bring our dreams to life.

Achieve your goals by bringing your dreams to life

STORM

The mood changes as a storm stirs.
The Dreamers are woken by an incessant, expectant rhythm as the sweet silence is shattered by the Wind Gremlins – the dark spirits who bring with them a furious gale that threatens to blow out the fires within us.

As the ferocious wind, horns and chanting whirl dramatically about our ears, the Dreamers battle to prevent the precious Agitos from rising adrift. Then suddenly an extraordinary, heroic motorcade of artists, creators, dancers, musicians and poets arrives to add their voice.

WIND GREMLIN

The sweet silence is shattered by an incessant, expectant rhythm

RAISING OF THE FLAG

HRH The Earl of Wessex
and
Sir Philip Craven
President of the International
Paralympic Committee
enter the Stadium

The circle is unbroken,
The ancestors awoken.
May the songs of the earth
and of her people ring true.
Hail to the Festival of the
Flame of root and branch,
tooth and claw, fur and feather,
of earth and sea and sky.

God save our gracious Queen!
Long live our noble Queen!
God save the Queen!
Send her victorious,
Happy and glorious,
Long to reign over us,
God save the Queen.

Thy choicest gifts in store
On her be pleased to pour,
Long may she reign.
May she defend our laws,
And ever give us cause,
To sing with heart and voice,
God save the Queen.
God save the Queen.
God save the Queen.

THE HEART OF MANY NATIONS

A flag day for hopes and hearts

This evening, we celebrate the 4,200 athletes from 164 nations whose exceptional endeavours and commitment to the Paralympic values – courage, determination, inspiration and equality – have captured our hearts and minds over the past 11 days.

Afghanistan · Albania · Algeria · Andorra · Angola
Antigua and Barbuda · Argentina · Armenia · Australia · Austria
Azerbaijan · Bahrain · Barbados · Belarus · Belgium · Benin
Bermuda · Bosnia and Herzegovina · Brazil
Brunei Darussalam · Bulgaria · Burkina Faso · Burundi · Cambodia
Cameroon · Canada · Cape Verde · Central African Republic
Chile · People's Republic of China · Colombia · Comoros · Costa Rica
Côte d'Ivoire · Croatia · Cuba · Cyprus · Czech Republic · Democratic People's Republic of Korea
Democratic Republic of the Congo · Denmark · Djibouti · Dominican Republic · Ecuador
Egypt · El Salvador · Estonia · Ethiopia · Faroe Islands · Fiji · Finland
Former Yugoslav Republic of Macedonia · France · Gabon · Gambia · Georgia · Germany
Ghana · Greece · Guatemala · Guinea-Bissau · Haiti · Honduras · Hong Kong, China
Hungary · Iceland · India · Indonesia · Islamic Republic of Iran · Iraq · Ireland
Israel · Italy · Jamaica · Japan · Jordan · Kazakhstan · Kenya · Republic of Korea · Kuwait
Kyrgyzstan · Lao People's Democratic Republic · Latvia · Lebanon · Lesotho · Liberia · Libya
Lithuania · Macao, China · Madagascar · Malaysia · Mali · Malta · Mauritania
Mauritius · Mexico · Republic of Moldova · Mongolia · Montenegro · Morocco · Mozambique
Myanmar · Namibia · Nepal · Netherlands · New Zealand · Nicaragua · Niger · Nigeria · Norway
Oman · Pakistan · Palestine · Panama · Papua New Guinea · Peru · Philippines · Poland
Portugal · Puerto Rico · Qatar · Romania · Russian Federation · Rwanda · Samoa
San Marino · Saudi Arabia · Senegal · Serbia · Sierra Leone · Singapore · Slovakia · Slovenia
Solomon Islands · South Africa · Spain · Sri Lanka · Suriname · Sweden · Switzerland
Syrian Arab Republic · Chinese Taipei · Tajikistan · United Republic of Tanzania
Thailand · Timor-Leste · Tonga · Trinidad and Tobago · Tunisia · Turkey · Turkmenistan
Uganda · Ukraine · United Arab Emirates · United States of America · Uruguay
US Virgin Islands · Uzbekistan · Vanuatu · Venezuela · Vietnam · Zambia · Zimbabwe
Great Britain

TRUCK INVASION

From a scrapyard of junk, a sensational motorcade is assembled by eager, industrious hands. Shaped by the imagination and powered by invention, it drives towards a new world of possibility.

Open your eyes and awaken your senses to a fresh future, shaking off the rust and dust, and rising phoenix-like from the welders' flames.

SPIRIT OF THE GAMES

Whang Youn Dai Award
Dr Whang Youn Dai, a tireless champion of the Paralympic Movement, presents awards to two athletes who've not only achieved sporting excellence, but exemplify the spirit of the Games – to inspire and excite the world.

IPC Athletes' Council
This evening, we recognise the six newly elected members of the IPC's Athletes' Council, who represent athletes within the Paralympic Movement and uphold their rights and obligations.

Volunteer Recognition
You don't have to win a medal to be a hero. Tonight, the athletes and all of us recognise the 70,000 Games Maker volunteers whose energy, enthusiasm and remarkable dedication has contributed to the success of London 2012.

COLDPLAY

When you've won adulation and acclaim the world over and sold more than 55 million records, you'd think life couldn't get much better. But for Coldplay, helping bring the curtain down on an unforgettable few weeks of sport that has captivated a global audience is about as good as it gets.

'We're a London band. We met here,' says lead vocalist Chris Martin. 'It's where we all record, rehearse and live. These Games have been a chance to show London off to the rest of the world – and for us to watch loads of table tennis!'

For Chris, Jonny Buckland (lead guitar), Guy Berryman (bass) and Will Champion (drums) there was no hesitation when they were approached to appear tonight. 'Kim Gavin came round to our studio… we signed up before he'd even finished the first sentence. Being asked to play at the Paralympic Closing Ceremony in our home town is a huge honour. We can't actually imagine a bigger honour. This will be the biggest night of our lives.'

'This will be
the biggest night
of our lives'

FESTIVALS

This evening's 'Festival of the Flame' pays tribute to the gatherings that infuse the spirit of our nation. We'll be reminded of the irrepressible power of music to draw us together, as it does at world-renowned festivals up and down the UK – from Kinross, Belfast and the Brecon Beacons to Glastonbury and the Isle of Wight.

As the circle of the seasons turns through the night, we'll also honour the elemental forces that shape each year and have been marked by our ancestors through spiritual rites and ceremony. And when all is done, we hope that the emotions that fill your heart – and you share with those around you – will be retold through generations.

The ancient seasonal cycle includes eight festivals, celebrated through the year. Four of them have Celtic origins and the other four are points in the solar calendar – spring and autumn equinox, summer and winter solstice. Ancient sites, such as Stonehenge in Wiltshire, act as gigantic solar calendars and show that festivals of the sun have been significant dates for thousands of years. The seasonal differences between the hemispheres mean solar festivals are celebrated six months earlier (or later) in the southern hemisphere.

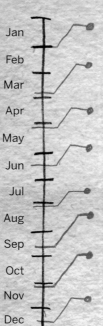

Jan
Feb
Mar
Apr
May
Jun
Jul
Aug
Sep
Oct
Nov
Dec

IMBOLC As we celebrate Candlemas, we know spring is on its way – its new shoots inspiring us to start planning new ventures.

OSTARA The days and nights are equal at the spring equinox, and light and warmth nurture growth and fertility.

BELTANE At the beginning of May, summer begins and we dance towards the sun, fired by the spirit of optimism for the plenty to come.

LITHA At the summer solstice, the sun reaches the height of its powers, the only shadow cast by the lengthening darkness each day.

LAMMAS The harvest is celebrated and bread made from the first crop at the beginning of August.

MABON The autumn equinox marks the point at which dark overcomes light. Life will leave the land and we must exist on the crops we harvested earlier.

SAMHAIN The supernatural and physical worlds draw closer at Halloween, and we prepare for the colder winter months to come.

YULE Winter solstice marks the turning point of our darkest season, when Mother Earth reawakens and the days increase in length.

AUTUMN

Summer's simmering sizzle makes way for the crackling fires of autumn. Clocks change and the harvest is gathered in. Thanks are given for the ripe, golden crop with a fiery tribute to the Sun King. Surrounded by flaming staffs that lick into the sky, he rises to signify the season's end.

'Up in flames
Up in flames
Up in flames'

UP IN FLAMES

WINTER

The warm shades of autumn fade to create a forest of frozen fantasy as we move into the darkest days of the year. Winter sees the Snow Queen released from her icy tomb and the landscape transformed with frozen thistles, amid a freezing magic carpet on which warriors skate and slide in their cold play.

Then from nowhere, the cacophonous revving of a throbbing beast shatters the season's frost-like grip. A revving motorcycle circles frantically out of the darkness. Gathering speed, its mystery rider collects a passenger. Up, up and away they soar, into the stratosphere, sparking the touchpaper that breaks winter's spell.

'There was snow, white snow'

VIOLET HILL

SPRING

Darkness switches to blinding light. Spring bursts forth and, lit by the solar glare, the earth's symbols are reborn. Forces of nature leap and spring into life, led by the vigour of youthful anticipation as the Car Kids join together with a new purpose. Now they're mechanics, and what was once junk and scrap, teems with their energy.

Summer is on its way.

'Confusion never stops,

closing walls and ticking clocks'
CLOCKS

SUMMER

The eternal cycle of the seasons completes another circuit with the arrival of summer. As our ancestors have done down the ages, we give thanks to the splendour of the sun; the warmth of its rays igniting our happiness. A community at one with itself, dancing dizzily round the maypole, rejoicing in the solar glare.

What was old, breathes life anew. Summer – a funfair for our hearts – is aflame again. Viva la vida... long live life.

'It's such, it's such a perfect day, it's such a perfect day'

STRAWBERRY SWING

ALÔ RIO

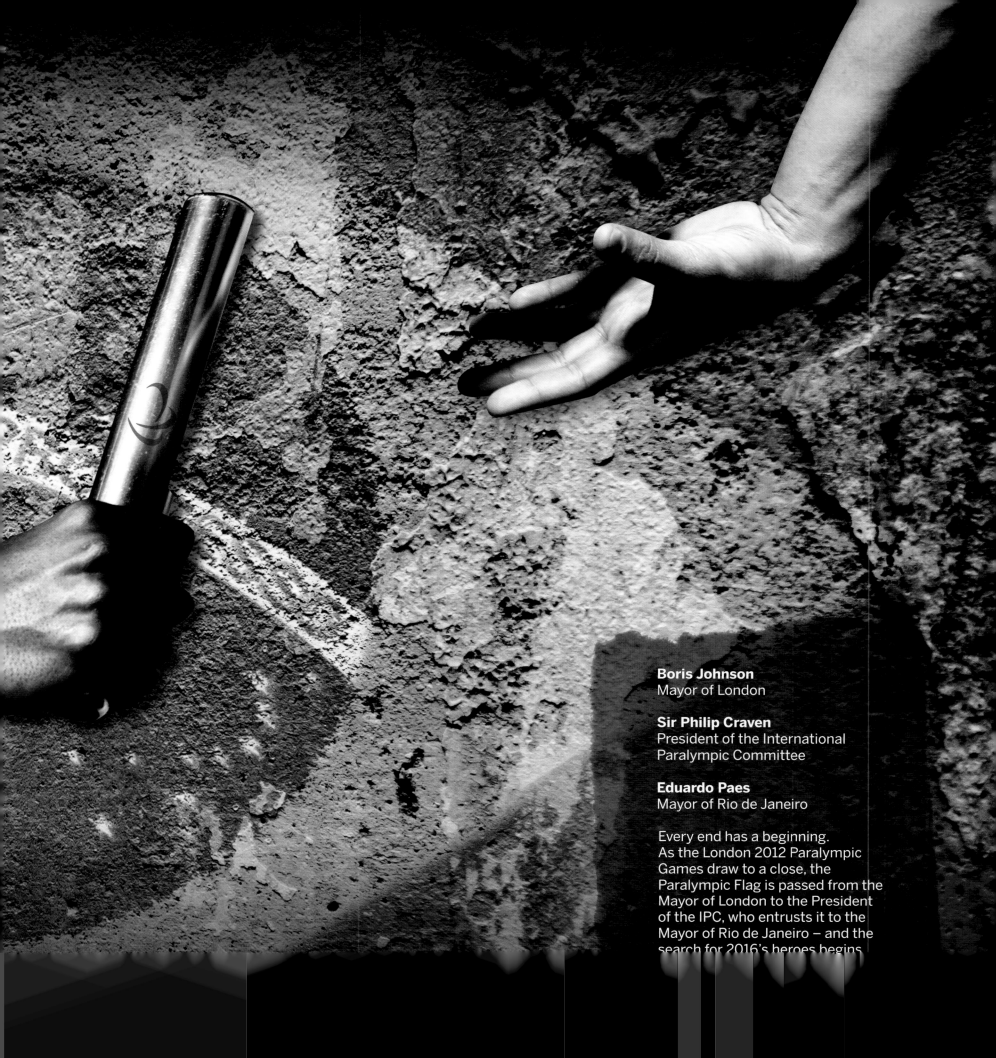

Boris Johnson
Mayor of London

Sir Philip Craven
President of the International
Paralympic Committee

Eduardo Paes
Mayor of Rio de Janeiro

Every end has a beginning.
As the London 2012 Paralympic
Games draw to a close, the
Paralympic Flag is passed from the
Mayor of London to the President
of the IPC, who entrusts it to the
Mayor of Rio de Janeiro – and the
search for 2016's heroes begins.

Joy

We are extremely proud to receive the Paralympic Flag tonight.

The Handover marks the first time a South American country will host the Paralympic Games. At this historic moment, we welcome the Flag on behalf of more than 190 million Brazilians.

The Rio 2016™ Paralympic Games will celebrate the athletes' determination and accomplishments. It will be an event full of humanity, which will bring people together and reinforce the perception that inside we are all the same. We share one heart that beats with the courage and strength of great achievements, spreading its positive energy around the world.

Come and celebrate the Rio 2016™ Paralympic Games. Share with us moments of inspiration and enthusiasm. It will be a memorable experience, highlighted by the colours and warmth of Rio de Janeiro. We welcome you to a city that wants to share its joy with the whole world.

Creative Directors
Cao Hamburger & Daniela Thomas
Creative Supervisor
Abel Gomes
Executive Producer
Marco Balich

THE FINAL FLAME

SPEECHES

Sebastian Coe
Chair, London 2012 Organising Committee
An authentic Olympic giant, Seb Coe won two
gold and two silver medals over successive
Games – 1980 and 1984. In 1979 he broke
three different world records in 41 days, and
his rivalry with fellow middle-distance runner
Steve Ovett is one of the great Olympic stories.

Sir Philip Craven
President, International Paralympic Committee
Philip Craven represented Great Britain at
Wheelchair Basketball at five Games, 1972-88.
Vastly experienced, both as an athlete and
progressive administrator, he received a
knighthood in 2005. This is his third Summer
Games since becoming President of the

Paralympic Flame

Twelve days ago, four flames travelled from the summits of the highest peaks in the four UK nations to Stoke Mandeville – birthplace of the Paralympic Movement – where they were united to create the London 2012 Paralympic Flame.

The following day, the Flame arrived in the Stadium at the Opening of the Games, carrying with it the spirit of the Paralympics and bringing the nations of the world together.

Burning bright noon and night across 11 days of sporting excellence, the Flame is now extinguished.

A powerful and poignant moment, it signifies the end of the London 2012 Paralympic Games and the countdown to Rio 2016.

FINALE

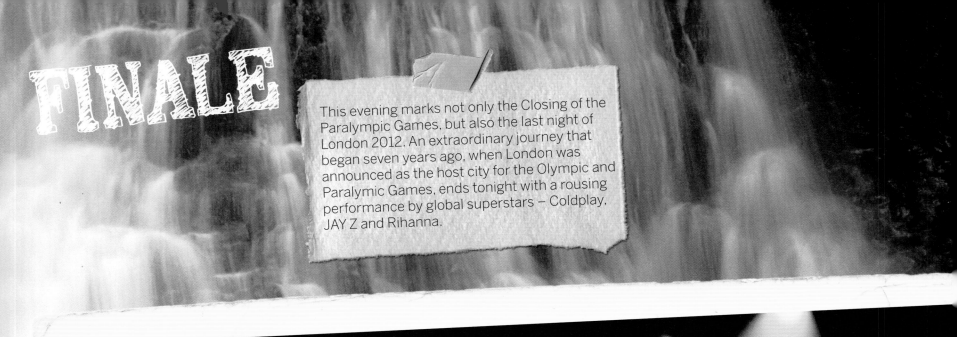

This evening marks not only the Closing of the Paralympic Games, but also the last night of London 2012. An extraordinary journey that began seven years ago, when London was announced as the host city for the Olympic and Paralymic Games, ends tonight with a rousing performance by global superstars – Coldplay, JAY Z and Rihanna.

Coldplay

As well as being one of the world's most acclaimed and bestselling music acts, Coldplay are active supporters of charitable causes, including Oxfam's Make Trade Fair, Amnesty International and Make Poverty History.

Rihanna

Since her debut in 2005, Rihanna has amassed an impressive six Grammy, 18 Billboard and two BRIT Awards. She's sold more than 37 million albums and 146 million digital tracks worldwide and this year was named 'one of the most influential people in the world' by *Time* magazine.

Fourteen-time Grammy Award winner Shawn 'JAY Z' Carter is an artist, songwriter, record producer and entrepreneur. He's dominated an evolution in music for more than a decade and, during his time as President and CEO of Def Jam Recordings, fostered the careers of international stars Rihanna, Ne-Yo and Kanye West. His philanthropic work includes the Water For Life initiative and the Shawn Carter Scholarship Foundation.

JAY Z

Who's Who?

You'll see thousands of talented performers this evening who've been working with hundreds of creative people behind the scenes to devise and deliver the London 2012 Paralympic Games Closing Ceremony.

Performers

Stadium Announcers
Trish Bertram
Marc Edwards

Dance Captains
Sarah-Jane Aboboto
Jennifer Chapman
Ciaran Connolly
Adrian Gas
Jared Hageman
Nathan Holliday
Claire Millin
Dougie Mills
Susan Shaw
Felicity Todd

Dancers
Kamilah Afiyah-Beckles
Cem Ahmet
Lucy Banfield
Big Grey
Simon Campbell
Shaun Capewell
Michelle Carter
Callum Clack
Scott Michael Coldwell
Tom Cunningham
Keely Dann
Gareth Davis
Micheal Downing
Erin Dusek
Layla Ellison
Martin Fenton
Luke Field-Wright
Leanne Hainsby
Crystal Hantig
Becky Hicks
Andrea Howarth
David Jamerson
Kate Kelly
Mandy Liddell
Oliver Metzler
Mandy Montanez
Shiloh Nelson
David Page

Chris Piper
Rohan Richards
Sarah Robinson
Brett Rosengreen
Paul Saunders
Craig Scott
Aaron Sillis
Lorraine Stewart
Bethany Rose Teagle
Laura Walker
Oliver Wheeler
Johnny White

Dreamers

Dream Squad Leader
Joe Dieffenbacher

Dreamers
Eric Adame
Simon Campbell
Jennifer Chapman
Ciaran Connolly
Micheal Downing
Adrian Gas
Kate Kelly
Dougie Mills
Chris Piper
Craig Scott

Dream Children
Hayley Downing
Bailey Nicklen

Storm

Wind Gremlins
Cem Ahmet
Gareth Davis
Luke Field-Wright
Nathan Holliday
Johnny White

Crows on Stilts Captain
Mark Tate

Crows on Stilts
Clare Barrett
Astra Beck
Delia Ceruti
Graeme Clint
Katherine Codogno
Gina D'Angelo
Jessica Harvey
Joe Hull
Scott Inskip
Michele Laine
Ms Merlin
Edward Muir
Alice Newton
Angelina Riley
Jen The Roo
Craig Sanderson
Adrian South
Tink
Emma Wellington

The Company Drummers
Danielle Bancroft
Sofia Bancroft
Carly Bourne
Joel Brogan
Lee Brogan
Ian Butt
John Calvert
Karen Calvert
Richard Cartwright
Bryn Cattell
Grant Cattell

Gemma Clarke
Lauren Cockburn
Nicola Cockburn
Adam Croft
Katie Dwyer
Dino Franchi
Nicholas Hankin
Phillip Hargreaves
Timothy Harper
Gillian Harrison
Luke Hawley
Claire Hein
Rebecca Hein
Ian Holling
Nigel Jackson
Thomas Jepson
Stephanie Kaye
Katy Kennedy
Georgia Kilshaw
Mark Long
Samuel Manger
Gregory Newbold
Jessica Newbold
Darren O'Meara
Helen Onions
Nathan Parker
Christopher Payne
Christopher Powell
Matthew Powell
Heather Rotchell
Nicole Safaei
Ashleigh Shearsby
Thomas Shepherd
Giorgia Sullivan
Wayne Sunderland
Maria Tarrant
Richard Taylor
Bekki White
Kirsty White
Alice Whiteley
Jack Whiteley
Sally Whiteley
Jordan Wright-Murray

Flare Carriers (H4H)
Staff Sergeant Elaine Corner
Private Derek Derenalagi
Jon Flint
Staff Sergeant Paul Gammon
Andrew Grant
Mark Lanchberry
Cornel Messam
David Scott
Erica Vey

Raising of the Flag

National Anthem Singer
Lissa Herman

Ministry of Defence Union Flag Team
Master Aircrew Attridge,
Royal Air Force, RAF High Wycombe
Guardsman Baleidraulu,
Army, 1 Coldstream Guards
Petty Officer Brown,
Royal Navy, HMS Collingwood
Leading Hand Bunnage,
Royal Navy, HMS York
Warrant Officer Burt,
Royal Air Force, RAF High Wycombe
Chief Petty Officer Grove,
Royal Navy, HMS Flying Fox
Marine Jackson,
Royal Marines, 30 Commando
Trooper O'Mahoney, Army,
Household Cavalry Mounted Regiment
Lance-Bombardier Peelo,
Army, King's Troop Royal Horse Artillery
Senior Aircraftman Rimmer,
Royal Airforce, RAF Leuchars
Corporal Robins, Army, 20 Transport
Squadron Royal Logistic Corps
Marine Timbs,
Royal Marines, 42 Commando

Royal Vehicle Driver (H4H)
Captain Tony Harris

The Company Drummers

Help for Heroes (H4H) Band of Brothers

Performers

Endeavour Flag Team (H4H)
Staff Sergeant Steven Arnold
Simon Brown
Bombadier Michael Browne
Lance Corporal
Martyn Compton
Ben Deakin
Corporal Claire Edwards
Andy Fisher
Private Iain Fuller
Corporal Ricky Furgusson
Senior Aircraftsman
Michael Goody
Corporal David Hubber
Jamie Hull
Kevin Juka
Marine Don MacLean
Lance Corporal
Peniasi Namarua
Barrie Newell
Lance Bombardier
Daniel Richards
Lance Bombardier
James Simpson
Captain Luke Sinnott
Private Craig Winspear

Reader (H4H)
Rory MacKenzie

Truck Invasion

Small-Vehicle Drivers
Helen Ball
Teresa Callan
Tina Carter
Tamlyn Clark
Vanessa Cook
Pippa Coram
Laura Cork
Colette Morrow
Vicky McManus
Sophie Page Hall
Amy Panter
Dela Seward
Robyn Simpson
Philippa Vafadari

Mother Earth
Mandy Liddell

Peacock
Shiloh Nelson

Astronomer
David Page

Dancers
Sarah-Jane Aboboto
Kamilah Afiyah-Beckles
Lucy Banfield
Big Grey
Shaun Capewell
Michelle Carter
Callum Clack
Scott Michael Coldwell
Keely Dann
Erin Dusek
Layla Ellison
Leanne Hainsby
Crystal Hantig
Becky Hicks
Andrea Howarth
David Jamerson
Oliver Metzler
Claire Millin
Mandy Montanez
Rohan Richards
Sarah Robinson
Brett Rosengreen
Susan Shaw
Lorraine Stewart
Bethany Rose Teagle
Felicity Todd
Laura Walker
Oliver Wheeler

Flame Oz
Grace Billings
Linda Blows
Thomas Johansson
David Knox
Dimitri Ogden
Jago Parfitt

Autumn

Candoco Dance Company
Darren Anderson
Laura Dajao
Dan Daw
Mirjam Gurtner
Annie Hanauer
Kimberley Harvey
Maggie Ho-Ki Kwan
Vicky Malin
Kate Marsh
Elinor 'Welly' O'Brien
Konstantinos
Papamatthaiakis
Susanna Recchia

Flame Dancers
Jennifer Chapman
Ciaran Connolly
Layla Ellison
Martin Fenton
Adrian Gas
Jared Hageman
Becky Hicks
Nathan Holliday
Susan Shaw
Aaron Sillis
Lorraine Stewart
Felicity Todd

Strap Act
Lyndsay Care
Denis Remnev

Winter

Aerial Fireflies
Katharine Arnold
Helen Ball
Teresa Callan
Tina Carter
Tamlyn Clark
Vanessa Cook

Pippa Coram
Laura Cork
Abagail Evans
Jo Foley
Louise Gibb
Natasha Hibbitt
Vicky McManus
Colette Morrow
Sophie Page Hall
Amy Panter
Jennifer Paterson
Dela Seward
Robyn Simpson
Philippa Vafadari

Snow Queen
Viktoria Modesta

Lead Warrior
Daniel Whiston

Blue Warriors on Skates
Matthew Evers
Mark Hanretty
Andrei Lipanov
Sean Rice
Lukasz Rozycki

Motorcycle Aerialists
Lyndsay Adams
Laszlo Simet

Spring

Butterflies
Eric Adame
James Booth
Ben Brason
Jack Helme
Dan Lannigan
Dan Liddiard
David Rimmer
Hasit Savani
Ben Smith

Ahmahd Thomas
Steve Williams
Charles Uezzell
Edward Upcott

Summer

Carousel Creature Flyers
Teresa Callan
Tamlyn Clark
Vanessa Cook
Pippa Coram
Laura Cork
Vicky McManus
Dela Seward
Robyn Simpson

Maypole Flyers
Helen Ball
Tina Carter
Colette Morrow
Sophie Page Hall
Amy Panter
Philippa Vafadari

The British Paraorchestra
Clarence Adoo
Abi Baker
Tilly Chester
Lloyd Coleman
Takashi Kikuchi
Adrian Lee
Lyn Levett
Gemma Lunt
Nicholas McCarthy
Christopher Melling
James Risdon
Baluji Shrivastri
Ziad Sinno
Matt Wadsworth
Stephanie West
Charlotte White
Charlotte White

Alô Rio

Paralympic Flag
& Brazilian Flag Team
(See Ministry of Defence
Union Flag Team)

Joy

Principal Performers
Carlinhos Brown
Thalma de Freitas
Daniel Dias
Roberta Marquez
Paralamas do Sucesso
Ádria Santos
Thiago Soares

Flame Oz

Candoco Dance Company

The British Paraorchestra

Ádria Santos, Carlinhos Brown, Thiago Soares, Roberta Marquez, Thalma de Freitas, Paralamas do Sucesso, Daniel Dias

Executive Team

Bill Morris
Director of Ceremonies,
Education & Live Sites

Bill joined London 2012 six years ago from the BBC where he started as a journalist, moved into radio and TV production and executive roles, before specialising in major events as Project Director Live Events. These included the BBC Music Live festival, the annual BBC Proms in the Park, the Olympic Torch Relay Concert in London's Mall, and the Queen's Concerts at Buckingham Palace (for which he was awarded the LVO in the Queen's Jubilee Honours List). He also coordinated broadcast live events across a number of BBC radio and television services, including Live 8 in 2005. Bill served on the Radio Academy's Council from the early 1990s, he was Chair 1998-2001, and was made a Fellow in 2001.

Martin Green
Head of Ceremonies

Trained in writing and directing theatre, Martin spent five years as Head of Events for the Mayor of London where he was responsible for producing global events such as the London New Year's Eve fireworks, major music festivals and one-off events across the city. As Director of Events at the O2 he oversaw the reopening of this now hugely successful venue. He joined London 2012 in 2007 as Head of Ceremonies, where he has recruited and inspired a world class team to deliver the Torch Relays, Victory Ceremonies, Team Welcome Ceremonies, and Opening and Closing Ceremonies of the Olympic and Paralympic Games.

Catherine Ugwu
Executive Producer, Production

Catherine is a creative director, executive producer and consultant and has been involved in some of the world's largest and most prestigious public events. She was Executive Producer for the Glasgow Handover Ceremony of the Delhi 2010 Commonwealth Games; Senior Producer for the strategic phase of the Opening, Closing and Victory Ceremonies of the 2010 Vancouver Winter Olympics; she produced the Opening Ceremony for the Asian Games in Doha, Qatar in 2006, the Closing Ceremony for the Commonwealth Games in Manchester in 2002 and a large-scale performance spectacle to mark the opening of the Millennium Dome, London in 2000.

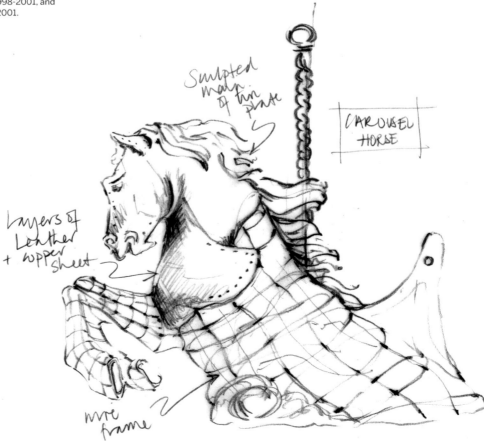

Stephen Daldry
Executive Producer, Creative

Stephen started his career at Sheffield's Crucible Theatre and directed extensively in Britain's regional theatres. In London he was Artistic Director of the Gate and Royal Court theatres; he's directed at the National Theatre, the Public Theatre in New York and transferred many productions to the West End and Broadway. His production of *Billy Elliot: The Musical* is currently playing in London and on tour in the USA. It recently won more Tony Awards (10) than any other British show in Broadway history. He's also made four films: *Billy Elliot*; *The Hours*; *The Reader*; and *Extremely Loud & Incredibly Close*.

Hamish Hamilton
Executive Producer, Broadcast/TV

Hamish, from Blackpool, is a Grammy nominated, multi-camera television and video director. He began his career as a trainee with BBC Scotland and as a TV director for the BBC Manchester Youth Programmes Unit. Pursuing his love of live music, he's directed the BRIT Awards, the MTV European Music Awards and the Victoria's Secret Fashion Shows for nine years. His credit appears on nearly 30 million live concert DVDs. His most recent work includes the Oscars, the MTV Video Music Awards and the Super Bowl halftime shows. He is also Creative Director of the television and event production company, Done and Dusted.

Mark Fisher
Executive Producer, Design

Mark's show design credits include *The Wall* for Pink Floyd in 1980 and Roger Waters in 2010; every Rolling Stones show since 1989 and every U2 concert since 1992. His architecturally innovative outdoor stages have been constructed several thousand times in cities all over the world. His event design credits include the Opening and Closing Ceremonies for the 2010 Commonwealth Games in Delhi, the 2010 Asian Games in Guangzhou and the 2008 Beijing Olympic Games. His theatre shows include *KÀ* and *Viva Elvis* for Cirque du Soleil in Las Vegas.

Artistic Team

Kim Gavin
Artistic Director

Kim is widely recognised as one of the UK's leading creative directors and choreographers. From one-off TV specials to record-breaking stadium shows, he's been the creative vision behind some of the most innovative and inspirational performances in the world of music and live events over the last 18 years. Kim trained at the Royal Ballet School and after a successful career as a dancer he turned towards choreography, stage and creative direction. Recent credits include Take That's critically acclaimed Circus and Progress Tours, Children in Need Rocks, and many individual artists' performances at the BRIT Awards and Royal Variety Performance.

Nathan Clarke
Associate Director

Nathan trained as a dancer in Australia and performed worldwide before moving into choreography. Choreography credits include Burlesque (Germany and France), The Overtones, Bananarama, JLS and, as Assistant Choreographer to Kim Gavin, Take That, Katherine Jenkins and Viva La Diva tours, The BRIT Awards and Royal Variety Performances.

Gareth Walker
Associate Director

Gareth's credits include creative director/choreography for Steps, Anastasia, Lulu, Chaka Khan and Mika; choreography for the Royal Variety Performance and the BRIT Awards; assistant choreography for Take That's Ultimate, Beautiful World and Circus tours; and show director for L'Oreal, Toyota and GHD. He's also presented and choreographed Ministry of Sound's fitness DVDs.

David Arnold
Music Director

David is a Grammy, BAFTA, Ivor Novello and RTS award-winning composer, songwriter and producer. Film scores include *Independence Day*, *Zoolander*, *Hot Fuzz* and five James Bond movies. He also works in theatre and television (*Sherlock*, *Little Britain*) and writes and produces with artists as diverse as Iggy Pop, k.d. lang and George Michael.

Misty Buckley
Designer

Misty's credits include large scale touring shows – Coldplay's Mylo Xyloto and Take That's Progress and Circus. She's designed sets for live arenas and televised music shows including Biffy Clyro, the BRIT Awards, T4 Stars and Bat For Lashes. Misty has been the creative director of The Park, and other areas at Glastonbury Festival, since 2007.

Michael Sharp
Costume Designer

Michael has designed shows and costumes for high profile productions, music tours and videos worldwide. Working from studios in England and France, his credits include Take That's Ultimate, Beautiful World, Progress and Circus tours, Darcey Bussell, Katherine Jenkins, Goldfrapp and the BRIT Awards.

Debbie Phillips
Producer

Debbie has produced and executive produced some of the biggest live music events around the globe. Highlights include producing the MTV Europe Music Awards for over seven years, live concerts with the biggest international acts, and non-music based events such as the Laureus World Sports Awards and Nickelodeon Kids' Choice Awards.

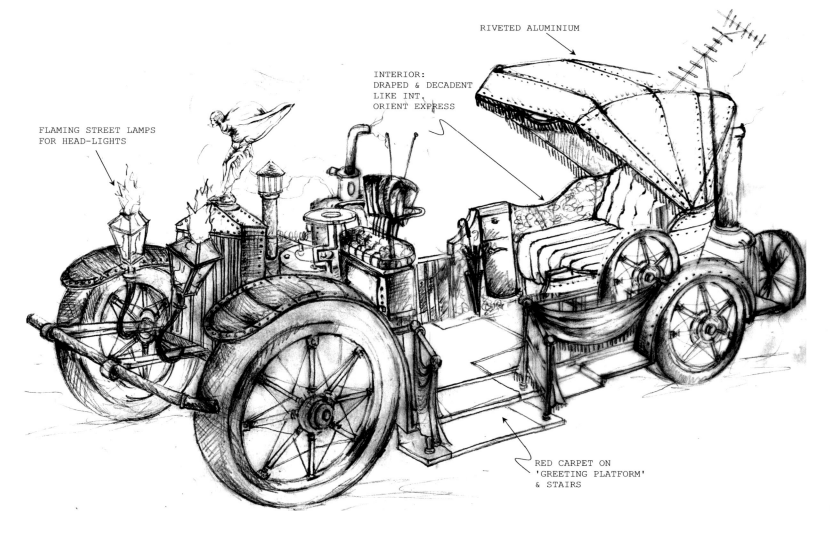

RIVETED ALUMINIUM

INTERIOR:
DRAPED & DECADENT
LIKE INT.
ORIENT EXPRESS

FLAMING STREET LAMPS
FOR HEAD-LIGHTS

RED CARPET ON
'GREETING PLATFORM'
& STAIRS

Production Team: Creative

Audio Design

Bobby Aitken
Audio Designer

Bobby is a world-renowned theatre sound designer. His work includes worldwide productions of *Ghost*, *Mamma Mia!*, *Dirty Dancing*, *We Will Rock You* and *Return to the Forbidden Planet*. Credits for large scale in-the-round opera include *Carmen*, *Madame Butterfly*, *Aïda*, *Cavalleria Rusticana* and *Pagliacci*, *Tosca* and *La Bohème*.

Scott Willsallen
Audio Systems Designer

Aerial & Special Skills

Phil Hayes Aerial & Special Skills Consultant
Alex Poulter Associate to Aerial & Special Skills Consultant

Audio Visual & Broadcast

Justine Catterall Head of Audio Visual
Adam Dadswell Presentation Manager
David Watson Digital Media Manager
Lizzie Pocock Audio Visual Department Coordinator
Lisa Brown Digital Media Assistant
Steven Harris Video Documentation

Graham Carlow Photographer
Matt Askem Video Screens Director
Tracey Askem Video Screens Production Assistant
Jane Jackson Broadcast Liaison Manager

Casting

Gillian Schofield Cast Manager, Professional
Sarah Chambers, Jane Salberg Cast Coordinators, Professional
Penny Davies Assistant Cast Coordinator, Professional & Volunteers
Rhian Davies Assistant Cast Coordinator, Professional
Sarah Murray Casting Assistant, Professional
Nicola Bouchard Company Manager

Sara-Ellen Williams
Cast Manager, Volunteers
Sara Berutto, Dianne Leach, Trish McClenaghan, Laura Windows
Senior Cast Coordinators, Volunteers
Michael Foley, Glenda Genovesi, Vanessa Griffiths, Helen Lam, Haitham Ridha
Cast Coordinators, Volunteers
Jenny Rogers Cast Coordinator, Schools
Cheryl Galbraith, Martin Malone, Kieran Shekoni Assistant Cast Coordinators, Volunteers
Hannah Caple Casting Assistant, Volunteers
Barbara Lisicki Access Manager

Costume, Hair & Make-Up

Tahra Zafar Head of Costume,
Hair & Make-Up
Alison Forbes-Meyler, Catherine Hill, Anna Lau
Costume Supervisors
Matthew George Hair & Wigs
Design Supervisor
Amber Sibley Make-Up Design Supervisor
Katie Newitt Costume
Department Coordinator
Lesley-Ann Halls Costume Department
Volunteers Coordinator
Caroline Brett Senior Costume Buyer
**Rebecca Mills, Samantha Langridge,
Charlotte McGarrie** Costume Buyers
Vanessa Bastyan Costume Workshop
Fabrication Supervisor
Angie Pledge Costume Workshop Supervisor
Robin McGrorty Costume Workshop
Senior Costumier
Thea Keenan
Costume Workshop Senior Fabricator
Nicola Beales
Costume Workshop Assistant
Maisie McCubbin
Costume Workshop Junior
Olima Rolfe Creative Division Assistant
Jamie Mendonça
Garment Stock Logistics & Driver

Lighting Design

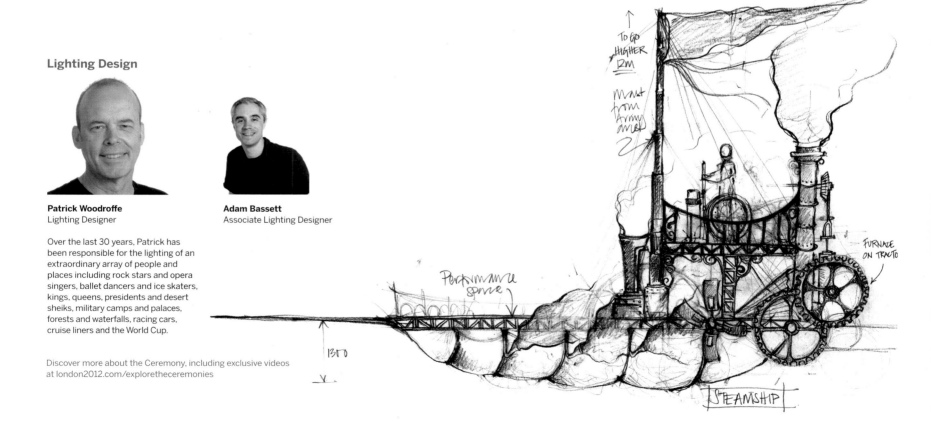

Patrick Woodroffe
Lighting Designer

Adam Bassett
Associate Lighting Designer

Over the last 30 years, Patrick has
been responsible for the lighting of an
extraordinary array of people and
places including rock stars and opera
singers, ballet dancers and ice skaters,
kings, queens, presidents and desert
sheiks, military camps and palaces,
forests and waterfalls, racing cars,
cruise liners and the World Cup.

Discover more about the Ceremony, including exclusive videos
at london2012.com/exploretheceremonies

Production Team: Creative

Mass Movement

Steve Boyd Head of Mass Movement Choreography & Parade of Athletes

Steve has contributed to 11 consecutive Summer and Winter Olympic Games from Barcelona 1992 to London 2012. Other credits include Special Olympics, Commonwealth Games, Cricket World Cup, Asian Games and Super Bowl halftime shows. Prior to event production, Steve designed for several Condé Nast publications including *Vanity Fair* and *The New Yorker*.

Soha Frem, Gina Chan Martinez, Rocky Smith, Nikki Woollaston, Nathan Wright
Mass Movement Leaders
Ben Clare, Laura-Anne Gill, Vicki Igbokwe, Jeanefer Jean-Charles, Natasha Khamjani, Katie Pearson, Barbarana Pons, Wendy Steatham
Mass Movement Coordinators
Edwina Allen, Taylor Anthony, Rachelle Conroy, Marianne Howard, Sean Mulligan, Brenda Jane Newhouse, Darragh O'Leary, Joseph Pitcher, Richard Pitt, Simone Sault, Carla Trim-Vamben, Claira Vaughan, Jayde Westaby
Mass Movement Assistants
Paul Neaum Manager, Parade of Athletes
Darrin Peters Assistant, Parade of Athletes

Design

Ala Lloyd Design Studio Manager
Emma Child Design Studio Coordinator
Basmah Arafeh, Rebecca Brower, Hatty Morris Design Studio Assistants

Music

Martin Koch Music Supervisor
Tom Jenkins Associate Music Supervisor
Clare Hazeldine Music Department Coordinator
Nick Gilpin Audio Supervisor
Toby Pitman, Rob Playford Music Programmers

Producers

Leon Campbell
Associate Producer

Leon's experience includes television production credits for all the major UK broadcasters on everything from large scale reality shows to music events and entertainment series. He was the Producer on the 2008 Handover for London 2012 in Beijing and part of the events team that re-opened The O2 in London in 2007.

Sarah Currie
Band Associate Producer
Annie Corrigan
Production Coordinator
& Protocol Manager
Hannah Davies
Personal Assistant
to Artistic Director
Kaz Hill Headline
Talent Manager
Sarah Casey Headline
Talent Coordinator
Danielle Buckley
Headline Talent
Production Assistant

Publications

Fiona Richards Publications Manager
Jess Anstee Publications Coordinator

Stage Management

Sam Hunter Production Stage Manager
Guido Foa Deputy Production Stage Manager
**Carola Altissimo, Liz Copp, Debbie Cronshaw,
Hilary Davis, Ben Delfont, Anthony Field,
Duane Harewood, Marianne Kuehner,
Claire Loftus, Jordan Noble-Davies, Sam Pepper,
Helen Smith, Ian Stephenson, Jorge Tapia,
Peter Wakeman, Matt Watkins**
Senior Stage Managers
**Holly Anderson, Miriam Bertaina, Abigail Dankwa,
Miguel de la Fuente Graciani, Rhiannon Harper,
Gareth Hulance, Bianca Jones,
Dominique Pierre-Louis, Ryan Quelch,
Kate Ramsey, Gemma Thomas** Stage Managers
Julia Whittle Show Caller

Video Content Design

Sam Pattinson Screen
Content Consultant Producer
Luke Halls Screen Content
Creative Director
Rhyannon Hanbury-Aggs
Screen Content Production
Manager

Creative & Executive Administration

Tina Jaffray
Senior Administrator, Creative
Jennifer Hutt Executive Assistant to the
Head of Ceremonies and Executive Producer
Kate Hinchliffe Executive Assistant
to the Producers
Nicky Cheung Personal Assistant to
Director of Ceremonies, Education & Live Sites
Veronique Haddelsey
Protocol Coordinator
Graham Gill Script Manager
Clare Ellis Administration Assistant
Lucy Moffat Runner
Tom Ford Driver

Internship Placements **Lexi Boynton, Andrew Clifford, Amy Gibson, Elizabeth Howe,
Katie Radha Osterholzer, Anisha Patel, Daniel Vincze**

Production Team: Technical

Technical Executive

Piers Shepperd
Technical Director

For 20 years, Piers has delivered technical production wizardry for mega events around the globe. Critically acclaimed projects in theatre and music include *We Will Rock You* and the Rolling Stones Licks World Tour. Other work includes the Athens 2004 Olympic Ceremonies, 2006 Doha Asian Games Ceremonies and 2010 Delhi Commonwealth Games Ceremonies.

Andrew Morgan
Senior Administrator, Technical
Elena Dogani
Production Coordinator,
Technical Contracts
Ross Nicholson
Production Assistant, Technical

Aerial & Special Projects

James Lee Technical Manager, Aerial & Special Projects
Glenn Bolton Senior Production Manager, Capital Works & Special Projects
Luke Mills Production Manager, Pyro, Flame & SFX
Edwin Samkin Deputy Production Manager, Pyro, Flame & SFX
Sammy Samkin Production Manager, Fireworks
Nick Porter Deputy Production Manager, Aerialist Training
Emma Neilson Production Coordinator

Audio, Comms & Broadcast

Chris Ekers Senior Production Manager, Audio & Comms
James Breward Deputy Production Manager,
Comms, CCTV & Mass Cast IEM
Alison Dale Deputy Production Manager,
Principal Performer IEM & Wireless Mics
Trevor Beck Audio Playback
Simon Honywill Audio FOH
Steve Watson Audio Monitor Engineer
Steve Williams Audio Broadcast Systems Engineer
Andy Rose Audio Broadcast Sound Supervsior

Lighting, AV & Power

Nick Jones Technical Manager, Lighting, AV & Power
Andy Loveday Senior Production Manager, Lighting
Ben Pitts Production Manager, Lighting Set LX
Dan Sloane Production Manager, Video & LED Screens

Tim Routledge Senior Lighting Operator
Lee Threlfall Set Lighting Production LX
Dave Bartlett Project Manager, Pixels
Mike Dawes Deputy Project Manager, Pixels

Staging & Scenic

Jeremy Lloyd Technical Design & Staging Manager
Steve Nolan Senior Production Manager, Staging, Scenic & Props
Nigel Mousley Senior Production Manager, Staging & Scenic
Steve Richards Senior Production Manager, FOP
Chris Clay, Dave Williams Production Managers, Staging & Scenic
Patrick Hocken Production Technical Stage Manager
Mike Grove Band Stage Manager
Kieran McGivern Deputy Production Manager, Staging & Scenic
Scott Seaton Deputy Production Manager, FOP
Daria Drazkiewicz, Johanna Eaden Production Assistants,
Staging & Scenic

Joe Rush Art Director, Mechanical Vehicles & Props
Oliver Brown, Andy Colby Production Coordinators
Simon Ambrose, Simon Lawrence Riggers
Tom White CAD Manager
Andrew Bailey, Ben O'Neill, Philip Wilding CAD Operators
Moose Curtis, Magnus Harding, Kevin Jones Staging Crew Chiefs
Peter English Head Carpenter
Phil Perry Staging Crew Chief, Rehearsal Venue
Ray Bogle Field of Play Crew Chief
Rasti Bartek, Aran Chadwick, Glyn Trippick Consultant Engineers
Richard Bentley, John Prentice CAD Consultants

Technical Services

Scott Buchanan Technical Manager,
Technical Services & Special Projects
Annette Stock Production Manager, Schedule,
Crew & Contractors
Jess Noakes Production Coordinator, Technical Services
Dave Wilkie Production Manager, Plant & AP
Matthew Beardsley Production Coordinator, Crew & Logistics
Terry Hubble Production Staff Quartermaster
Laura Lloyd, Grant Peters, Chris Tani Production Staff Runners

Workshop & Props

Ted Irwin Technical Manager, Workshop & Props
Dan Shipton Production Manager, Props
Pam Nichol Deputy Production Manager, Props & Rehearsals
Eric Hickmott Production Manager, Workshop
Hannah Charlesworth, Rhiannon Newman-Brown
Deputy Production Managers, Props
Nick Bloom Deputy Production Manager, Carpentry
Sherri Hazzard Deputy Workshop Manager, Props
Sally Christopher, Sean Flynn Production Coordinators, Props

Internship Placement Laura Rixson

Richard Olivieri Props Art Director
Mark Moore Deputy Production Manager, Metal Fabrication
Will Sumpter Deputy Workshop Manager, Props
Steve Dart, John McGarrigle Props Electricians
John Pratt Workshop Coordinator & Buyer
Dave Blacker Props Coordinator and
Crew & Volunteer Chief
Stephen Jeffrey Crew & Volunteer Chief
Krissy Lee Technical Assistant

Production Team: Operations

Operations Executive

Mik Auckland
Director of Operations and Health & Safety

A career as a stage manager and technical director in musical theatre led Mik to senior roles at the Sydney 2000 and Athens 2004 Olympic Games. In 2005 he joined Jack Morton Worldwide as Senior Technical Director. Mik subsequently worked on the Beijing 2008 Olympic Games and the 2010 FIFA World Cup as Consultant Technical and Operations Director.

Adrian Bourke Senior Manager, Venues & Facilities
Joseph Frisina Senior Operations Manager
Donna McMahon Senior Manager, Logistics
Neil Russell Senior Manager, Health, Safety, Welfare & Medical
Hannah Dorey Senior Administrator, Operations
Nathan Farquharson Logistics Coordinator
Jacinta Gee Operations Coordinator
Luke Woodham Venues & Facilities Coordinator
Alice Larmer Logistics Production Assistant

Health, Safety, Welfare & Medical
Show Operations & Scheduling

Conrad Schwarz Deputy Manager, Health & Safety
Sally-Ann Dod Health & Safety Advisor, Inductions & Contractor Liaison
Sarah Jones Medical Services Manager
Danielle Bromley, Steve Brown, Alan Law Health & Safety Consultants
Samantha Coles Coordinator, Health & Safety
Sally Downey Health & Safety Inductions Assistant
Dean Jewel Show Operations & Schedule Manager
Paddy Bettington Show Operations & Schedule Assistant
Leah Harris, Sam Mount Schedule Production Assistants

Logistics

Kirsty Thomson Operations Manager,
Catering, Cleaning & Waste
Julia Bowditch, Lynsey Jackson Coordinators, Catering,
Cleaning & Waste
**Rebecca Fletcher, Sandra Goetz, Gareth Lewis,
Ria Maycox, Alexander Thomas, Sarah Yates**
Production Assistants, Catering, Cleaning & Waste
Melissa McVeigh Operations Manager, Accreditation
Melanie East, Tyler Ffrench, Vincenzo Ianniello
Coordinators, Accreditation
Karen Cosgree, Emily Whitaker
Production Assistants, Accreditation
Laura Marakowits Operations Manager, Volunteers
Shelly Donaghy Coordinator, Volunteers
Grace Birkbeck, Laura Salvatore, Pete Thomson
Production Assistants, Volunteers
Valie Voutsa Operations Manager,
Accommodation & Travel
Leticia Gonzalez-Galvez Assistant Manager,
Accommodation & Travel (Principal Performers)
Eloise Crevier, Eirini Zoi
Production Assistants, Accommodation
Georgina Huxstep Operations Manager, Transport & Fleet
Sarah Hinchelwood Assistant Manager, Children's Transport
Matthew Howlett Assistant Manager, Fleet & Site Vehicles
Kate Blomfield, Asha Slade Coordinators, Transport
**Simon Galicki, Laura Gallen, Charlotte Howley,
Emma Lester, Emily Webber**
Production Assistants, Transport
Debbie Paul Operations Manager,
Principal Performer Logistics
Craig Lear Green Room Manager
Anna-Maria Kreuzer Coordinator,
Principal Performer Logistics
Victoria Sandford, Ed Woodhouse
Production Assistants, Principal Performer Logistics

Venues & Facilities

Russel Bedford Operations Manager,
Workshop & Rehearsal Venues
Pete Williams Assistant Manager,
Rehearsal Venues
William Francis Coordinator, Workshop
& Rehearsal Venues
Sonya Gandras Coordinator, Rehearsal Venues
**Billy Cheeseman, Ralph Cullum,
Charlotte Jordan** Production Assistants, Venues
Robert Madeley, Isabel Uriach Site Assistants,
Rehearsal Venue
Lucinda Erskine-Crum Operations Manager,
Olympic Park
Al Parkinson Assistant Manager, Olympic Stadium
Toni Stockham Coordinator, Olympic Stadium
David Gregory Assistant Manager, Compound
Marcia Connell, Will Gunnett
Coordinators, Compound
Robert Schnaiberg Assistant Manager,
MDS, Storage & Freight

Sarah Adams, Olivia Pole-Evans
Site Assistants, MDS, Storage & Freight
Lottie Cresswell Assistant Manager,
Common Domain
Chui-Yee Cheung Coordinator,
Common Domain
Ryan Tate Coordinator, Venue
Lily Sutton, Tanisha Malkki
Production Assistants, Venue
Eva Budd, Holly Gregory
Compound Assistants,
Stadium

Internship Placements Bryony Mitchison, Dimitry Ragozin, Charlotte Ryan

Production Team: Administration

Administration Executive

Sara Donaldson
Joint Chief Operating Officer

Sara has overseen the delivery of many high-profile events and campaigns, including the bid for London 2012. In 2000 she set up LIVE Communications and was awarded an OBE. She co-founded Unspun in 2008 with whom she led the strategic direction of England's bid for the 2018 FIFA World Cup and co-produced the Glasgow 2014 Commonwealth Games Handover in Delhi.

Chris Laue
Joint Chief Operating Officer

A key team member from the beginning of London 2012 Ceremonies, Chris has served as Procurement and Contracts Director, Board Director, Producer and Interim Chief Operating Officer. Prior to moving to London, he was Creative Producer/Director for LiveCity Vancouver, the city's live sites for the 2010 Olympic and Paralympic Winter Games.

Finance

Colin Blessley Finance Director
Andrew Slater Financial Controller
Veronica Bailey Management Accountant
Kathleen Anderson Production Accountant
Mladen Ivezic, Farishta Yousuf
Senior Purchase Ledger Administrators

Human Resources

Rebecca Janiszewska Human Resources Manager
Geraldine Daly, Cherise Scotland, Derek Taylor Human Resources Coordinators
Selina Donald Executive Assistant to Chief Operating Officer
Chidimma Chukwu Finance, Payroll & HR Clerk

Internship Placement Christianne Gandossi

Information Technology

Campbell McKilligan
Head of IT & Comms
Dilraj Sachdev Database Manager
Gyula Keresztely-Krall
System Administrator
Grant Cassin Mac Specialist

**Saif Ahmed, Abdullah Al-Mamoon,
Regis Joffre, Rica Mackay, Irfan Mohammed,
Khizzar Younis** Desktop Engineers
Marita Samuel IT Department Coordinator
Mick Turvey Service Desk Manager

Legal

Will Hutchinson Head of Legal (Culture,
Ceremonies, Education & Live Sites)
Chris Loweth Senior Ceremonies Lawyer
Shirin Foroutan Senior Ceremonies
Legal Advisor
Sarah Naisby Trainee Solicitor
Rachael Barrows Assistant
Company Secretary

Procurement & Contracts

Simon Aspland
Head of Procurement & Contracts
**Natalie Foster, Robert Graham, Ilyas Rahman,
Stephanie Tillman, Marlon Trotman**
Procurement & Contracts Administrators

Monique Pennycooke, Rachel Williams
Procurement & Contracts Coordinators
David Sugden Lawyer

Ceremonies, Education & Live Sites

Caroline Ainley Financial Control Accountant
Anna Blackman Programme Manager
Mark Smith Finance Manager
Kristina Richmond Procurement Manager

London 2012 Ceremonies Ltd

Scott Givens
Managing Director

Scott is an Olympic Ceremonies and mega-event
producer with more than 300 spectaculars to his
credit. Leading the team at creative production firm
FiveCurrents, he has worked on 11 Olympic Games,
and was awarded the prestigious Olympic Order. His
productions have also received numerous Emmy
Awards, Telly Awards and Sports Business Awards.

Board of Directors

Scott Givens (Chair)
Sara Donaldson
Martin Green
Chris Laue
Bill Morris
Catherine Ugwu
Frank McCormack (non-executive)
Alan Robertson (non-executive)

London 2012 Ceremonies Committee

Bill Morris (Chair)
Charles Allen
Doug Arnott
Jackie Brock-Doyle
Seb Coe
Paul Deighton
Martin Green
Will Hutchinson
Catherine Ugwu
Neil Wood

Production Credits

Special Thanks

AgustaWestland
Arts Council England
BMW
British Fashion Council
Crystal CG
Dr. Martens
GoPro
Massey Ferguson
Samsung
Signature Systems Group
Site-Eye Time-Lapse Films
Swarovski
Trekinetic
Tumblr

Acknowledgements

3 Mills Studios
Flying Pictures
Help for Heroes
Omer Ali
Warrant Officer Barker
Charles Hazlewood
Amanda Softly

Access Team
Jacqui Beckford
Martin Fox-Roberts

Assistant Stage Managers
Eleanor Butcher
Grace Cameron
Stuart Campbell
Shaun Corcoran
Henrietta Curtis
Anthony Earles
Chloe French
Gemma Friel
George Hims
Scarlett Hooper
Osnat Koblenz
Tom Leggat
Dan Miller
Connor Mitchell
Zanna Orage
Georgia Paget
Christopher Mark Smith
Philippa Sutcliffe
Sarah Sweet
PK Thummukgool

Audience Pixel Content
Created by Crystal CG
Ben Alderman
Daniel Balzer
Fillipo Bianchi
Daniel Capstick
Will Case
Ed Cookson
Liam Corner
Giedre Domzaite
Neil Evan
Henry Flitton
Ed Fyfe
Jude Greenaway
Robert Grieves
Jayne Hobart
Jing Huang
Jason Leigh
Al Liddell
Giles Maunsell
Andrew McKinna
Jessica Morgan
Gideon Prins

Chris Ratcliffe
Jamie Shiels
Zsuzsanna Voros

Audio Visual
Sim Canetty-Clarke
Tom Moss
Max Tipple

Casting
Perform Health Physiotherapy
Paul Adams
Genevieve Baker
Steve Brownlie
Maz Bryden
Janet Care
Marc Cass
Graham Downing
Nicola Downing
Rebekka Evans
Joanna Griffith
Cassandra Harris
Sainbold Janchivdorj
Ellena Jones
Pedro Machado
Andrea Mangena
Leigh Nicklen
Stine Nilsen
Adrian Porter
Diana Prociv
Lesley Raymer
Craig Sherratt
Solomon Wilkinson

Costume
Acton Cut
Nicola Kileen Textiles
Whaleys
Helena Bennett
John Cowell
Andy Farrow
Jane Gill
John Handley
Georgina Lamb
Daniel Marks
Fiona Parker
Susanne Parkinson
Janita Patel
Ingrid Pryor
Rupert Sanderson
Kay Symons
Nikki Trelvean
Vivienne Westwood

Costume, Hair and Make-up Specialist Crew
Sarita Allison
Nikki Belding
Elisabet Berggren
Jennifer Bernard
Rachel Buxton
Sylvaine Champeau
Katy Cherry
Charlie Cooper
Andrea Cracknell
Alexina Duncan
Ian Denson
Liam Farrelly
Leon Fernholdt
Pam Foster
Oliver Gamblin
Mandy Gold
Gemma Hoff
Lizzie Judd
Alexandra Kharibian
Shelley King
Spencer Kitchen

Charlotte Lander
Melanie Lenihan
Monica MacDonald
Catherine McCloughlin
Kirsteen Naismith
Emily Newbold
Jo Nielsen
Jess O'Shea
Rose Octon
Amy Sachon
Katharine Scott
Margarida Santos
Emma Slater
Mariella Spoto
Elaine Solomon
Helen Spink
Kerry Spring
Dianne St James
David Stringer
Janine Summerhayes
Wendy Topping
Jo Tuplin
Gemma Vincent
Laura Watkins
Nicola Webley
Laura Wisinger
Jenna Wyatt

Design
4D modelshop
Georg Fischer Piping Systems
London Graphic Centre
Chris Blyth
Reg Matheson
Milk
Tea Mulabdic
Paris
Sayaka Takeuchi

Finance
Albert Goodman LLP
IT Associates Ltd

Human Resources
Beder-Harrison & Co
Vikki Gee-Dare
John Wilson

Information Technology
Adobe
Electranet
Jigsaw 24
Lesar
Netapp
Symantec
Allan Whatmough

Legal & Clearances
Department for Education
Michael Simpkins LLP
Universal Music
Nion Hazell
Kate Penlington
Barbara Zamoyska

Mass Movement
Polly Bennett
Bryn Walters

Music
Air Studios
Dakota Music Ltd
London Symphony Orchestra
Chris Barrett
Alison Burton
Dave Hage
David William Hearn

Sue Mallett
Kathryn McDowell CBE
Marc Stevens
Nick Wollage

Operations
British Waterways
Bunzl
Cabots
The Civil Aviation Authority
Corinthia Hotel
Ford Dagenham
Gravis Capital Partners LLP (GSP)
Grosvenor Facilities Services Ltd
Hyatt Regency London - The Churchill
IDS Develop
JLAB
JLAR
London Borough of Barking and Dagenham Council
London Development Agency
NATS
Sam's Cars
Sanofi
Sheraton Park Tower
West One

Procurement
Bravo Solutions

Props Specialist Crew
Theo Cresser
Helen Hall
Mark Morley Smith
Angela Pettit
Philip Quinn
Kay Symons
Marc Wardley
Gin Warren
Laura Woodroffe

Task Force 27
Including representation from:
Government Olympic Executive
Greater London Authority
London 2012 Ceremonies Ltd
London Organising Committee of the Olympic & Paralympic Games Ltd
London Rail
London Underground
Metropolitan Police Service
Network Rail
Transport for London
Westminster City Council / London Councils

Technical
A Plant
Adler and Allan
Ainscough Crane Hire
Arcadia
Artem
Atelier One
Banks Sails
Bruce Banks Sails
Buro Happold
Carbon Lighting
Creative Technology
Delta Sound
Elstree Light & Power (ELP)
EMPA
ER Productions
FCT Flames

Fibreweb Geosynthetics
Fineline
Flying FX Ltd
Gallowglass
Howard Eaton Lighting
H-Squared Electronics
Jason Lane
Kimbolton Fireworks Ltd
Kinetica
Land Development Services
Linemark
Media Share T/A ER Productions
Mutoid Waste Company
MTFX Ltd
Paul Liengaard
Pixel Poi
Power Logistics
PRG
Quantum Special Effects
Riedel Communications
Segway Events
Serious Stages
Sheetfabs
Showforce
Showstars
Stage One Creative Services Ltd
Star Events Group
Steel Monkey Engineering
Tait Technologies
The Technical Department
Total Fabrications
Transam Trucking
Trike Design
Unusual Rigging Ltd
Water Sculptures
WiCreations
Will Trickett Boats

Technical Specialist Crew
Guy Aldridge
Colin Armitage
Gibson Arpino
Hamish Bamford
Natasha Bingham
Malcolm Birkett
Francesca Boyle
Dan Evans
Dario Fusco
Jason Gilbert
Jamie Hogan
Linford Hudson
Cattrina Mott
Nick Mumford
Rebecca Nelson
Jem Nicholson
Mike Pattison
Chris Patton
Ali Pretty
Michael Scott
Pauline Stone
Jamie Taylor
Chris Tidmarsh
Zoe Walker
Rachel Walsh
Richard Wearing
Oliver Welsh
Robert Woodley

Vehicle Makers
Andrew Borghs
Lulu Butcher
Thomas Cherry
Toby Coe
Ian Coiley
Cath Coppock

Dave Farrington
James Gallagher
Justin Grant
Charles Harrison
Liam Hayhow
Ross Hogan
Ian Ingram
Felicity Jones
James Kearney
Thor Laslett
Daniella Lewin
Tom Mansell
Tom McAlaster
Simon Murray
Phil Neil
Frances Plowden
Gareth Price
Charley Robarts-Arnold
Jamey Robshaw
Pand Stamp
Micha Sztalryd
Steave Tesla
Neil Thompson
Matthew Webb
Alex Wright

Broadcast & Film

Broadcast
Channel 4
CTV Outside Broadcast
Done & Dusted
Presteigne Charter

The Book of Fire
Mike Christie
Tom Evans
Megan Hill
Rachel Naughton
Luke Palmer
Claire Parkinson
Eddie Sears
Mark Talbot-Butler

Music Credits

Welcome
David Arnold, Toby Pitman,
Andy Treacey
Written by Arnold

Wind / Storm
London Symphony Orchestra,
David Arnold,
Chris Baron, Paul Clarvis,
Toby Pitman, Andy Treacey
Orchestrated & conducted by
Nicholas Dodd
Written by Arnold

National Anthem
Performed by Lissa Herman

Life in Technicolor
Coldplay,
Urban Voices Collective
Written by Berryman/
Buckland/Champion/
Martin/Hopkins
Universal Music Publishing Ltd
/Kobalt Music Publishing
Master courtesy of
EMI Records Ltd

Politik
Coldplay
Written by Berryman/
Buckland/Champion/Martin
Universal Music Publishing
Master courtesy of
EMI Records Ltd

Burning the Field
London Symphony Orchestra,
Urban Voices Collective,
David Arnold, Chris Baron,
Paul Clarvis, Andy Treacey
Orchestrated & conducted by
Nicholas Dodd
Written by Arnold

Us Against the World
Performed by Coldplay
Written by Berryman/
Buckland/Champion/
Martin/Eno
Universal Music
Publishing Ltd / Opal Music

Yellow
Performed by Coldplay
Written by Berryman/
Buckland/Champion/Martin
Universal Music Publishing Ltd

Up in Flames
Performed by Coldplay
Written by Berryman/
Buckland/Champion/Martin
Universal Music Publishing Ltd

Paradise
Performed by Coldplay
Written by Berryman/
Buckland/Champion/
Martin/Eno
Universal Music
Publishing Ltd / Opal Music

Violet Hill
Performed by Coldplay
Written by Berryman/
Buckland/Champion/Martin
Universal Music Publishing Ltd

42
Performed by Coldplay
Written by Berryman/
Buckland/Champion/Martin
Universal Music Publishing Ltd

God Put a Smile on Your Face
Performed by Coldplay
Written by Berryman/
Buckland/Champion/Martin
Universal Music Publishing Ltd

Clocks
Performed by Coldplay
Written by Berryman/
Buckland/Champion/Martin
Universal Music Publishing Ltd

Charlie Brown
Performed by Coldplay
Written by Berryman/
Buckland/Champion/
Martin/Eno
Universal Music
Publishing Ltd / Opal Music

Princess of China
Performed by Coldplay, Rihanna
Written by Martin/Berryman/
Buckland/Champion/
Birgisson/Dyrason/Holm/
Sveinsson/Eno
Universal Music
Publishing Ltd / Opal Music

Strawberry Swing
Performed by Coldplay,
The British Paraorchestra
Written by Berryman/
Buckland/Champion/Martin
Universal Music Publishing Ltd

We Found Love
Performed by Coldplay, Rihanna
Written by Harris
EMI Music Publishing

Viva La Vida
Performed by Coldplay
Written by Berryman/
Buckland/Champion/Martin
Universal Music Publishing Ltd

Paralympic Anthem
Performed by
The British Paraorchestra
Arranged and conducted by
Charles Hazlewood
Written by Darnis

Run This Town
Performed by Coldplay,
JAY Z, Rihanna
Written by Riddick/West/Festy/
Carter/Wilson/Alatas/Alat
EMI Music Publishing Ltd /
BMG Music Publishing /
SonyATV Music Publishing /
Warner Chappell Music
Publishing Ltd

The Scientist
Performed by Coldplay
Written by Berryman/
Buckland/Champion/Martin
Universal Music Publishing Ltd

Every Teardrop is a Waterfall
Performed by Coldplay
Written by Berryman/
Buckland/Champion/Martin/
Castioni/Christensen/
Lagonda/Allen/Anderson/
Wycombe/Eno
Universal Music Publishing
Ltd / Warner Chappell Music
Publishing / Opal Music

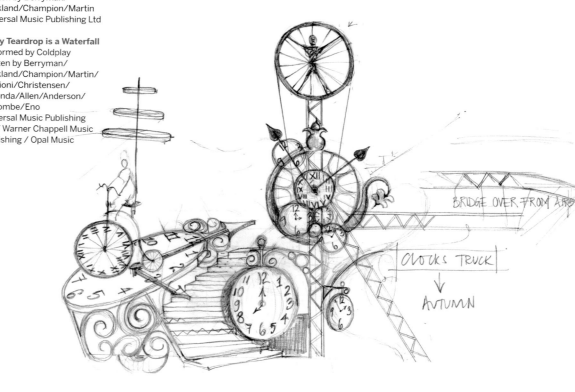

BRIDGE OVER FROM ARCH

CLOCKS TRUCK

AUTUMN

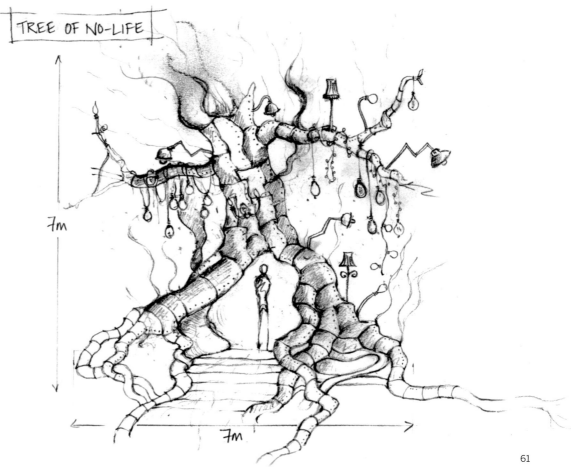

TREE OF NO-LIFE

7m

7m

Clearance Credits

General

Getty Images
Heroic speech based on the Gorsedd Rite
by Emma Restall Orr and Philip Shallcrass

Programme

Alamy
Corbis
Getty Images
Andy Hall
Simon Hayward
Cover design by Heatherwick Studio
International Paralympic Committee
iStock
Sarah Lee/Eyevine
NASA
Chris Nurse@Debut Art
Paris 1974
Katherine Rose
Jamie Sage
Sawmarlar
Andrew Shaylor
Shutterstock
John Swannell/Camera Press
Andrew Zaeh/ Zaeh LLC
Jurgen Ziewe@Debut Art

Accessibility

We're committed to inclusive working practices for artists, staff and collaborators, and want this evening's Ceremony to be an enjoyable experience for everyone.

Audio-description

If you have a visual impairment, you can pick up a free audio commentary device from one of the London 2012 Information Points in the Stadium (there are four around the concourse). If you're sighted and interested in experiencing audio description, you can buy a radio for £6 from the Programme and Commentary Radio sellers.

British Sign Language Interpretation and Captioning

BSL interpretation and/or captioning are relayed on the Stadium screens when there is spoken word in the Ceremony.

Mobility

Games Mobility is a free service for disabled spectators. If you require a manual wheelchair, mobility scooter or assistance to your seat, please ask a Games Maker or at an Information Point:
Zone E2 (opposite Block 128)
Zone A (opposite Block 138)
Zone B (opposite Block 146)
Zone C (next to Bridge C)

Programme

If you'd like this programme in another language or format please email info@enquiries.london2012.com or phone +44 (0)845 267 2012 quoting LOC2012/CER/1423.

Please ask a Games Maker – one of those nice people in the purple and red tops – if you have any questions or require assistance.

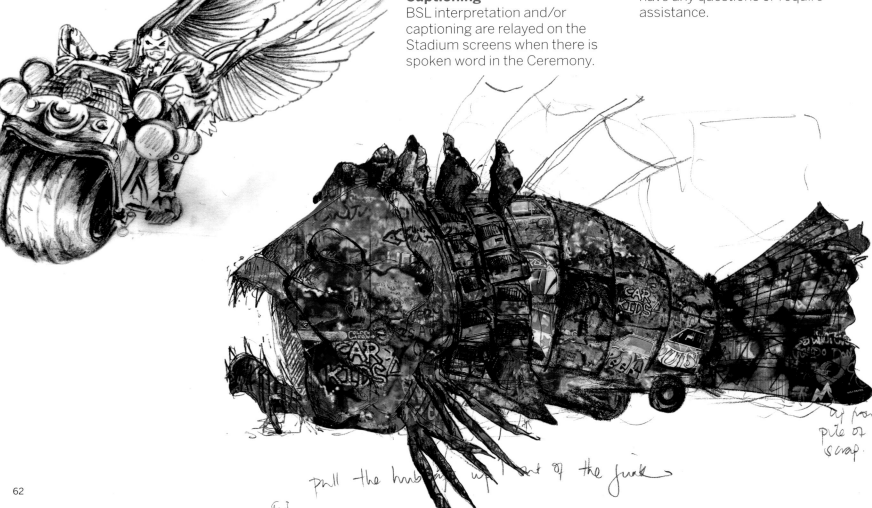

Audience Pixel Screen

Published under license from London 2012 by Haymarket Network, Teddington Studios, Broom Road, Teddington, Middlesex TW11 9BE. Tel +44 (0)20 8267 5000. Reprinting in whole or in part is forbidden except with prior permission of the publisher. Due care is taken to ensure that the content of this programme is accurate, but the publisher and printer cannot accept liability for errors, omissions or alterations. Additionally, Ceremonies Producers acknowledge the contribution of anyone involved in the Ceremony whose name does not appear in the programme due to publication deadlines. Any alterations or additions to the credits will be available online at london2012.com/exploretheceremonies.

Printed at an environmentally aware ISO14001 printer on FSC® certified paper.

This programme and the official emblems of the London 2012 Games are © London Organising Committee of the Olympic Games and Paralympic Games Limited. All rights reserved.

FSC
www.fsc.org
MIX
Paper from responsible sources
FSC® C013417

The London 2012 Olympic and Paralympic Ceremonies are a celebration of, and a showcase for, 21st-century technology. Among the most exciting new ideas is the ground-breaking 'audience pixel screen', designed and built especially for the Ceremonies.

The system has been realised by a number of organisations, but the core vision and expertise sits within the London 2012 Ceremonies team. Piers Shepperd, Head of Technical, says 'The pixel screen extends around the seating area and is made up of 70,799 small panels mounted between the seats. Each of the panels has nine LED pixels – that's nearly 640,000 in total, each controlled by a central computer. Using a variety of techniques, including stop-motion and CGI animation, the screen displays amazingly complex and beautiful images that flood the Stadium'.

'We were incredibly excited to have the opportunity to work on such a wonderfully immersive digital project. The scale and challenges involved in getting the most from the innovative technology required a team of more than 50 experts to design 100 plus original pieces of animation', says Ed Cookson from Crystal CG, the company who created the visual content.'

Spectators have also played a vital role in bringing the Artistic Directors' vision to life in each of the four Ceremonies. Encouraged to pick up the panels and move them around, the audience have become an integral part of the cast.

Who can forget the Union Jack rolling out across the seating area as 'the Queen' parachuted in, at the Olympic Opening Ceremony; the immersive audio-visual experience of the Olympic Closing Ceremony; and the golden dandelion seeds that accompanied the lighting of the Cauldron at the Opening of the Paralympics? They'll live in the memory of audiences both in the Stadium and at home for a long time, and you can expect some more breathtaking effects this evening.

CAROUSEL SWAN

Saddle for performer

Layers of lace + tin

Painted muslin + cardboard tail

wire frame

Volunteers

Pre-Show & Dreamers Asad Abdullah, Adelaide Afrides, Michelle Agyakwa, Doreen Agyei, Shelim Ahmed, Ann Ahmed, Atiya Ahmed-Sheikh, Indera Ajimal, Mosunmola Akanji, Addy Akinbami, Adunni Akindude, Lara Akpojiyovwi, Imad Al Dakkak, Towhid Bin Alam, Kelly Al-Dakkak, Annette Alexander, Salmah Ali, Glen Allan, Susan Allport, David Allum, Amonn Al-Mahrouq, Anandi Amin, Dilesh Amlani, Beverley Amoah, Faye Andrews, Kate Angel-Page, Monifa Angus, Korantema Anyimadu, Naoko Aoyama-Beard, Deepthi Aricatt, Sophie Ashdown, Hifzah Asif, Paul Astbury, Patricia Attwell, Alex Badrick, Amanda Bailey, Anthony Bailey, John Bainton, Pathmanathan Balaskanthan, Steve Ball, Allan Ballesteros, Patricia Baran, Isabel Barbuk, Lynn Barker, Lucy Barnes, Daisy Barnett, Denise Barr, Diana Barrett, Jane Bartlett, Sally Barton, Ursula Barzey, Constance Barzey-Browne, Alison Basa, Hulya Bayraktar, Michael Beard, Khiltee Beeharry, Zohra Bekhadra, Conrad Benjamin, Valeria Bettini, John Beveney, Kenny Beveridge, Sana Bhadelia, Kirthi Bhat, Christine Bignold, Sarah Bingham, Sonia Birchall, Katerina Biszko, Louise Blinn, Cydatty Bogie, Lydia Bolwell, June Bonfield-Brown, Rhiannon Brace, Trisha Bradley, Nigel Brinklow, Hannah Broad, Penny Brookman, Emma Broomfield, Annabelle Brouquisse, Camilla Brueton, Glen Bryan, Katie Bryer, Jolanta Bujauskiene, Jenny Bunclark, Katie Bunting, Gemma Burrows, Ammar Butt, Margaret Byrne, Claire Callender, Marie Calvert, Annie Campbell, Sean Campbell-Hynes, Christy Carey, Jane Case, Maria Casey, Isabelo Castillo, Judit Castillo-Barta, Aviva Cerner, Keith Chong, Ann Charles, Devashish Chatterjea, Parbhu Chauhan, Nisha Chavda, Zhuoyu Chen, Peggiann Chevailler, Brandon Chin, Jane Chinery, Edna Chirwa, Athikur Rahman Choudhury, Inun Nahar Chowdhury, Man-Hua Chu, Susie Clapham, Justin Clapton, Ella Clark, Maria Clark, Anabel Claro Garcia, Hannah Coates, Wendy Coath, Jessica Cobb, Niel Cogle, Bianca Cole, Hilary Cole, Emma Collins, Rebecca Comerford, Marine Conan-Clement, Emelda Conroy, Eve Conway, Lis Cook, Declan Cooke, Paul Cooke, Penny Costa, Anne Costello, Julie Cotterill, Liz Couper-Johnston, Colin Coxall, Bex Crisp, Cheryl Crombie, Victoria Custerson, Patricia Cutler, Gillian Dacey, Carmen Dacres, Tom Dale, Giovanni Dalla-Valle, Shauna Daly, Leaphia Darko, Tej Pratap Daswani, Jill Davies, Larry Davies, Mark Davies, Amelia Dawson, Jacqueline Day, Silvia Maria De De Mello, Elizabeth Dean, Jody De'Ath, Amanda Decktor, David Dee, Edwin Dela Cruz, Emma Delgado-Martinez, Anne Mary Demidowicz, Emel Deniz, Mariya Derelieva, Michelle Devall, Brigitte Dingle, Martina Dobrikova, Deedee Doke, Ebony Dormer-Kuti, Imran Dosani, Siobhan Draper, Angela Duguid, Gwyneth Duhy, Georgina Dumler, Megan Louise Dumphreys, Wendy Dunn, Jennifer Dutton, Matthew Dyson, Kara Earl, Myles Earle, Rebecca Edwards, Patricia Ehiorobo, Anna Eka, Clive Elkington, Sophie Embury, Georgia Emm, Louise England, Jeanette Eniola, Rachel Erickson, Fatima Evans, Margaret Evans, Bess Fairfax, Catherine Farmer, Susan Farnsworth, Carol Felton, Tatiana Fernandez Cardozo, Jessica Ferris, Marie Figueiredo, Liz Findlay, Emmanuel Finndoro-Obasi, Sally Fisher, Roy Fitchew, Nathalie Fitzgerald, Jacky Fleming, Katie Floyd, Ian Foley, Paolo Fornasiero, Wendy Forrest, Rebecca Foster, Yvonne Fox, Eilidh Fraser-High, Arnold Frazer, Carmencita Frosch, Demelza Fry, Emma Fuller, Chinye Furner, Carol Gadsden, Malcolm Galea, Ej Gamboa, Pallvi Gami, Renu Gangooly, Claire Gardiner, Sonja Garsvo, Fatumata Gassama, Elena Gattinara, Christopher Gavin, Ian Gedge, Belinda Gee, Eva Georgieva, Lyn Gibbins, Pauline Gilhooly, Alexandra Gill, Nicole Gipps, Sharon Gleave, Annie Gleeson, Sarah Goddard, Sandeep Gohil, Graciete Gomes De Pina Costa, Jennifer Gondola Bokoba, Serena Gonsalves-Fersch, Joanie Goss, Marilyn Gould, Jennifer Goulden, Ben Goulding, Nelson Grant, Jane Grant, Linda Gray, Michelle Graydon, Anthony Green, Janice Green, Steve Greenslade, Anne Gregory, Andrea Greve, Evelyn Griffiths, Laura Grist, Matilde Guerriero, Yosheeta Gunamal, Weiwei Guo, Hannah Guppy, Anil Gupta, Kie Haddow, Laura Hagger, Sue Haggerty, Helen Haile, Alice Hall, Carol Hall, Charlotte Hamilton, Lynsey Hamilton, Katie Hammond, Marie-Claire Hancock, Mari Hansen, Daniel Harding, Elaine Hargreaves, Nicole Harmar, Zena Harris, Kadia Harrison, Miranda Harrison, Stephen Harrison, Pru Harrold, Shelley Hart, Michelle Hawkins, Terry Hayden, Mark Hayman, Carole Hayward, Felicity Hearn, Jo Heath, Mo Henderson, Kim Henderson, Anna Henry, Catherine Henshaw, Tom Herbert, Lindsay Hettrick, Grace Hewitt, Jan Hickman, Anna Hirst, Sarah Hixson, Judy Ho, Rebecca Hoath, Philippa Hobbs, Amy Hodgins, Sarah Hole, Marica Holliday, Cynthia Holness, Veronica Hooles, Kate Horne, Julie Horwood, Christine Houghton, Sarah Houghton, Beverley Howes, Stephen Howson, Michelle Hsieh, Ting Hu, Ting Huang, Anna Hughes, Meleta Huie-Drummond, David Hume, Jake Hurlock, Josue Hurtado, Amran Hussain, Shaon Hussain, Sari Huttunen, Daniila Iaremko, Jojo Ibegbuna, Inemesit Imoh, Lara Inge, Victoria Innes, Katia Ivanchenko, Claire Jackson, Lorna Jackson, Susie Jackson, Annette Jaggard, Dan Jakob, Andrea James, Aubrey James, Sunny Jaspal, Isobel Jayawardane, Angela Jelfs, Rickie Jennings, Christine Jimenez, Sophie Johannot, Joely Johnson, Andrew Johnston, Andrew Jones, Clare Jones, Doreth Jones, Jane Jones, Margaret Jones, Val Jones, Beverley Jordan, Judith Joseph, Roshini Joseph, Grzegorz Junka, Ayoola Kabara-Clarke, Monika Kalde, Anu Kalyanji, Isata Kamara, Anita Karklina, Farhana Karmali, Kornelia Karweta, Abul Kasam, Anisha Kaur, Jill Keating, Eoin Kelly, Elaine Kelso, Teresa Kennedy, Kanji Kerai, Raynee Keshav, Muhammed Khan, Kamal Khaveripour, Tashfeen Kholasi, Anne King, Denise King, Ed Kingscote, Caroline Kirkpatrick, Mary Kisuge, Lisa Kliszat, Melanie Knoedler, Laura Koonjean, Ursula Kopp, Paul Kowald, Bogdana Kozhuharova, Chris Krishnan, Chanique Kyra-Jadewaithe, Nadia Laice, Amitabh Lall, Lynne Lambert, Alison Lamothe, Nyree Lane-Watkins, Paulina Lara Franco, Janek Lasocki, David Lathwell, Elaine Lau, Rebecca Launchbury, Lucy Leach, Josie Ledesma De Thorn, Je-Woo Lee, Tim Lee, Julia Lee, Helen Leighs, Roberta Lenart, Jane Leonard, Camilla Leonelli, Sok Leong, Amalthea Leung, Fiona Lewis, Leonie Lewis, Claudine Lewis, Dez Lewis, Carole Leybourne, Ge Li, Liaoyuan Li, Yi Li, Ying Li, Steven Linden, Sophie Littler, Hilary Lloyd, Michelle Lo, Clare Long, Fiona Lord, Gemma Loughhead, Connie Low, Lyn Lua, Barbara Ludlow, Michael Wai Ko Lung, Julie Lung, Louisa Lynagh, Katharine Lynch, Rachel Lyons, Jing Ma, Elizabeth Macintyre, Katie Mackinnon, Peter Magee, Hillary Malcolm, Rajinder Marbay, Tony Marie, Brian Marks, Karen Marks, Sharon Marshall, Alexandra Martin, Pamela Martin, Wendy Martin, Natalia Martinez, Amina Mashkas, Shilpa Mathuradas, Anthea Maton, Ausilia Matraxia, Sally Maxwell, Camilla Mayer Baird, Jacqueline Mayston, Ajay Mazumdar, Kelley McGiff, Sarah-Jo McClellan, Tansy McCluskie, Fiona McCormick, Rebecca McCullough, Samantha McDonough, Chloe McGregor, Angela McIntosh, Conor McKeown, Hugh McLaren, Katherine McLean, Beverley McNichols, Kathryn McPherson, Gaynor Mead, Gemma Mears, Isabella Mees, Shaheen Meghji, Hema Mehta, Roshni Mehta, Vrinda Mehta, Dom Melaragni, James Messer, Ramona Metcalfe, Charlene Michael, Lina Michael-Imobioh, Jane Michele, Inge Midl, Cristina Mihaiescu, Christine Millington, Sally Mills, Pam Milsom, Terry Minshaw, Chris Minton, Roberta Miozzi, Jasu Mistry, Jonathan Mitchell, Mary Mitchell, Catherine Moat, Jasvir Singh Modaher, Sara Mohammed, Anne Molloy, Natalie Mooney, Hannah Moore, Lesley Moore, Hannah Morgan, Emma Morris, Carmel Morrissey, Gerlin Moses, Linda Moss, Sarah Mujinya-Motima, Abbie Munk, Cristina Munteanu, Sharlene Nair, Rosemin Najmudin, Bruntha Narendran, Kate Nash, Lindsey Neil, Patricia Newman, Sovra Newman, Hor Yien Ng, Margaret Ngui, Joan Nicolaou, Tim Noble, Ryan Noel, Aicha Noui, Aileen Nurse, Elaine Nutton, Emma O'Brien, Wendy O'Brien, Pauline Odlin, Caroline Odogwu , Louise Offer, Cheryl O'Garro, Olukemi Ogunyemi, Idris Ogunyomi, Miriam Okarimia, Rachel Okarimia, Michele Olphonce, Abi Orebiyi, Louisa Orr, Emily O'Sullivan, Steve Outram, Sameera Oye, Susan Page, Jeshad Palkhiwalla, Beverley Palmer, Carolyn Panday, Gloria Parilli, Jonathan Partridge, Neringa Paskeviciute, Reena Pastakia, Chandrika Patel, Dini Patel, Jyoti Patel, Risha Patel, Shobhana Patel, Lynne Paterson, Phillip Patricks, Manju Patwari, Rebecca Pavlik, Jennifer Payne, Martin Payne, Sam Peachey, Robert Pearson, Wendy Pendle, Charlotte Pereira, Alison Perry, Theresa Peterson, Eva Petrou, Stefano Philand-Maini, Andrea Phillips, Jean Phillips, Paul Phillips, Kirstin Phillipson, Trudi Pickin, Angela Pillay, Xiaolan Ping, Shaun Pledger, Henry Poh, Karin Pointner, Glenn Pollard, Monika Pomeroy, Julie Poole, Joanne Powell, Sian Priest, Anna Pritchard, Ann Pruce, Martina Puchberger, Gemma Putney, Kat Quantrill, Nadia Quigley-Lewis, Sonal Raghwani, Faizur Rahman, Md.Azizur Rahman, Heenal Raichura, Vinoh Raja Gopal, Sahitha Rajendra, Anita Rajput-Havell, Ruby Rall, Anne Ramon, Bhabinder Rana, David Rasiah, Sarah Ratford, Vimlesh Ravalia, Sheik Raymode, Vanessa Redmond, Sarah Reeve, Lisa Remedios, Ginie Ribadeau Dumas, Marilena Ricciardi, Cheryl Richardson, Hannah Richbell, Angela Riches, Carissa Rickeard, Andrew Rivera, Carlene Roberts, Kenneth Roberts, Alice Robinson, Sinead Rocha, Lelia Roche-Kelly, Louise Rodway, Joanne Rook, Chloe Rooney, Ana Maria Rosales Hernandez, Maria Rosiak, Leslie Ross, Denise Roudette, Hannah Rouse, Deborah Rowe, Sanchita Roy, Vicky Royall, Helen Rufai, Shirley Ruiz, Sandhya Ruparelia, Izabela Ruprik, Amy Russell, Betty-Ann Russell, Caroline Russell, Chloe Russell, Lucy Russell, Lesley Ryan, Christina Sage, Kaltrina Sahiti, Gogi Saini, Peter Salter, Mercedes Samavi, Genine Sambile, Don Samkange, David Sanchez, Herjotpal Kaur Sandhu, Ashley Sandsmith, Dhanisha Sanghrajka, Raphael Sanglay, Buledy Sangwa, Philippa Sant, Claire Sargent, Francoise Sargent, Sandie Sargent, Hayley Saywood, Lizzie Scales, Anika Schwarz, Phil Scotton, Lorayne Seaholme, Margaret Searle, Ethel Senior, Felix Serkis, Hinal Shah, Nel Shah, Niranjana Shah, Shrida Shah, Aishatu Shaibu, Xiao Shan, Richard Shand, Trudy Sharman, Hilary Sharpe, Steve Shaw, Helen Shead, Yangyang Shen, Lisa Shepherd, Nigel Sheppard, Jessica Shiel, Genevieve Sibayan, Jackie Sibthorp, Maria Sierra-Negrete, Charlotte Silva, Spencer Simmons, Mandy Simpson, Monique Simpson, Anthony Smith, Chloe Smith, Emily Smith, Jeremy Smith, Paul Smith, Rob Smith, Susan Smith, Valerie Smith, Lauren Smithers, Barry Smyth, Cienna Smyth, Sandip Sodhi, Olu Sonuga, Luisa Sotgiu, Riyo Sovi, Margaret Sparkes, Ruth Spencer, Dennis Spencer-Perkins, Ann Spratley, Karoline Stanton, Karen Stead, Phillip Steadman, Ally Steele, Kay Steele, Daniel Stephenson, Elizabeth Stevenson, Hayley Stewart, Joanna Stratton, Rose Streatfeild, Carlene Street, Janet Ann Sullivan, Katherine Sullivan, Christine Sutton, Csilla Szeles, Arshad Takun, Rebecca Talsma, Chung Tim Grace Tang, Graham Tann, Jessica Tatnell, Denise Taylor, Kishore Taylor, Patricia Taylor, Yue Teng, Ruth Teverson, Ann Thain, Bharat Thakore, Renuka Thakore, Hellen Thatcher, Alastair Thomas, Bitu Thomas, Lucy Thompson, Martina Thompson, Sharon Thompson, Bee Thorkildsen, Amanda Thorne, Michael Timms, Aileen Toal, Naomi Tobias, Manisha Toprani, Frances Touch, Connie Tough, Angela Tregaskes, Liene Treimane, Louisa Trickett , Monia Troislouche, Andrea Turner, Lorna Turner, Shreena Turner, John Turrell, Laura Tutty, Adebisi Twins, John Tyler, Georgie Tyrrell, Su Tysoe, Mehreen Umar, Michel Varela Morales, Kaja Variku, Natalie Verbo, Laura Viander, Athena Vince, Greer Vincent, Jenny Vincent, Ekatierina Vorontsova,

Volunteers

Gaurang Vyas, Angela Wade, Penny Wai, Mark Wainwright, Andy Wakeford, Kathryn Wales, Joanne Walker, Samantha Walker, Janet Walter, Baiyu Wang, Xiaojue Wang, Yidai Wang, Judith Ward, Marilyn Ward, Hazel Ware, Lynne Watson-O'Neill, Richard Watts, Thomas Wearne, Steven Webb, Oriel Weekes, Andrew Welsh, Jing Wen, Tracey Wessels, Jeanne Whalen, Will Wheeler, Rebecca Whitehead, Lettice Wigby, Ruth Wilkinson, Mary Wilkinson, Pauline Williams, Peter Williams, Tracey Williams, Jane Wilson, Sheila Wilson, Rebecca Wilson-John, Maxine Wingrove, Mary Winmill, Avenell Winston, Shui-Yee Wong, Sue Wood, Janelle Wyke-Joseph, Emily Wynne, Xiaojun Xie, Ray Yates, Iris Yau, Jennifer Yaxley, Farhana Yeasmien, Wei Lit Yew, Rosalind Zeffertt, Cen Zhang, Yani Zhang, Ying Zhang, Xiaohong Zheng, Tommi Zhou, Min Zhou. **Storm** Louise Adams, Pritika Agarwal, Shawn Aldin-Burnett, Danielle Allen, Anita Anin-Boateng, Oliver Ayling, Aaron Bailey, Mikesh Bassi, Yvette Bezuidenhout, Jack Bishop, Hannah Bown, Lynnette Boyes, Scott Bryan, Justin Caesar, Oliver Carmichael, Emily Carpenter, Rachael Carter-Eagleton, Kitty Castledine, Lucy Castledine, Stewart Castledine, Yue Chen, Daniel Cope, Elizabeth Cordingley, Gill Coverdale, Helen Curtis, Laura Deane, Robert Duncan, Lindsey Elkins, Daria Emery, James Farrimond, Sarah Forster, Matthew Fox, Svetlana Garkusha, Elizabeth Hall, Nicolas Hardy, Vicky Hedley, Marlene Hell, Sophie Hocking, Mengjie Hu, Jade Louise Ireland, Lee Johnson, Hayley Jordan, Alex Kay, Ameeta Kerai, Krzysztof Krzemianowski, Harmesh Kumar, Erika Kuster, Peter Laurie, Doug Lloyd Haynes, William Martin, Thomas Maskell, Carel Meganck, Rachel Morley, Emma-Louise Negus, Kristin Parrish, Barbara Petgrave, Gaya Pillai, Lucina Ridgwell, Mary Robinson, David Sharpe, Scott Slaytor, James Tait, Charmaine Thomas, William Tweddell, Jonathan Tyson, Mrudula Venkatachalam, Sofia Vranou, Doreen Walford, Laura Warner, Vicky Hedley, Naomi Worth. **Raising of the Flag** Steve Arnold, Simon Brown, Michael Browne, Martyn Compton, Elaine Corner, Ben Deakin, Derek Derenalagi, Claire Edwards, Andrew Fisher, Jon Flint, Iain Fuller, Ricky Furgusson, Paul Gammon, Mike Goody, Andrew Grant, Mark Harding, Tony Harris, David Hubber, Jamie Hull, Kevin Juka, Mark Lanchbery, Rory MacKenzie, Don MacLean, Cornel Messam, Peniasi Namarua, Dan Richards, Dave Scott, James Simpson, Luke Sinnott, Erica Vey, Craig Winspear. **The Heart of Many Nations** Adejoke Abudu, Blessing Aladetoun, Javier Albarracin Perea, Charles Albert, Shelina Alleebux, Simonne Allen-Mason, Adem Andress, Marius Antanavicius, Mandy Ashmore, Jennifer Baker, Steve Ball, Mutiya Balogun, Jie Bao, Tim Baros, Poppy Begum, Alexandre Benedito, Dav Bisessar, Helen Bolger, Fabiola Bonnot, Fatima Boudafcha, Sally Bradshaw, Lennox Brown, Rheiss Brown, Nicola Burnett, Juliet Cahill, Magdalena Chalupnik, Mark Champion, Pin-Hsiu Chen, Kate Chia, Helen Coates, Sophie Colbourne, Chris Collier, Josie Coster, Rodney Da Silva, Paul Degnan, Kevin Deyna-Jones, Yvonne Dockery, Xianhui Dong, Erica Emm, Katie Evans, Melanie Farquharson, Hana Gajdosova, Long Gan, Lexie Gill, Ally Gomes, Reema Hooks, Michael Gonzalez, Jessica Guilding, Maria Hamalainen, Richard Harris, Stephen Haskins, Fang He, Edward Hellewell, Brad Hepburn, Henry Herrera, Ailsa Hewitt, Wayne Hincks, Robert Hunt, Baber Hussain, Victoria Irving, Rebecca Ison, Chyna Izundu, Jey Jeyakumar, Rebecca Jones, Martin Jones, Vanessa Jubenot, Giedre Kalvaityte, Jazz Kalyan, Kamal Kamal, Kiran Kara, Armenoui Kasparian Saraidari, Thalinga Keerthiratna, Georgina Kenlock, Jahanzeb Khan, Layla Khoja, Imelda Koch, Demetrios Komodromos, Ramaswami Krishan, Margaret Labongo, Sara Laratro, David Lee, Nicola Lees, Thomas Lennon, Diane Leung, Li Li, Shuyuan Li, Yang Li, Mei Lim, Zhen Lim, Sylvia Lu, Xiaomin Luo, Chloe Ma, Martin Malone, Geoff Manley, Antonie Marie, Dan Mayer, Hiwot Mendahun, Anish Mistry, Caroline Mistry, Aye Moe, Dave Nattriss, Ania Neuman, Tom O'Boyle, Jeremy Okai, Letycia Oliveira, Stan Onyejekwe, Inka Oshodi, Krishanth Paskaran, Krupali Patel, Sanjay Kumar Hasmukhlal Patel, Tom Peters, Jez Phillips, Louise Phillips, Andrew Plum, Lee Powell, Carlos Quinteiro, Jo Regis, Magnus Reinvik, Victoria Riley, Letticia Roberts-Clarke, Carol Robinson, Jenny Robinson, Imogen Rolfe, Gemma Ronte, Ilaria Rovera, Laura Ruthnum, Anna Sabin, Cleofe Sagun, Sanish Sambasivan, Dominique Sapsin, Michele Saviano, Stuart Savill, Nathan Saviour, Andrew Severs, Kieran Shekoni, Anusheel Shrivastava, Philip Slade, Georgie Smith, Hayley Smith, Jessica Smith, Dhanu Sobhanan, Qian Song, Alastair Steele, Kemi Sulola, Karinlolita Takacs, Grace Tang, Nora Tawfiq, Stephanie Taylor, Mary Thompson, David Threadkill, Justine Thrower, Paul Torry, Emma Triner, Terry Truong, Vinod Unadkat, Aneeka Vasa, Charlotte Verrill, Isabelle Veysey, Magali Villiot, Loriana Vitillo, Eleonora Vuorinen, Waithe Waithe, Nazina Webb-Thomas, Rhiannon Wilds, Danielle Willemsen, Priscilla Williams-Kofoworade, Roger Winfield, Katey Wood, Amanda Woods, Sarah Woods, Louise Woodward, Mark Wootton, Boleslaw Wroblewski, Gilbert Wu, Oren Yefet, Hon Mo Yip, Shayan Zahid, Shu Zhang, Yaxin Zhang, Duanyang Zhao, Yidan Zhu. **Truck Invasion** Emily Bagshawe, Seema Bassi, Stephanie Beckford, Ray Bennett, Sandra Bennett, Dominic Betts, Ajay Bhandari, Alastair Blackburn, Harriet Blain, Benjamin Boatman, Jonathan Booth, Richard Brass, Kristen Callaway, Sean Canning, Michael Carter, Emily Charles, Periyasamy Civagnanam, Michelle Clarke, Clare Cody-Richardson, Richard Cooper, Sanheeta Dighé, Adeline Doxaran, Chloe Edwards, Michael Ellis, Susannah Evans, Christine Fauvette, Celia Findlay, Catherine Foreman, Helen Foster, Arabella Gourlay, Agris Graveris, Margaret Gray, Claire-Louise Greenaway, Trude Hagenauer-Ringer, Peter Hall, Cherie Huang, Christopher Humphries, Jade Johnson, Tom King, Debra Knight, Paul Langton, Elizabeth Laryea, Gabrielle Leith, Christopher Lockey, Dorothy Luke, Soloman Makaddar, Joseph Maksymowicz, Nicolas Marsden, Stephen Marsh, Kurt Mayers, Jason Millington, Andrew Morris, Alexandra Mostyn, Richard Murray, Samson Ng, Lorna Oates, Samuelson Obigbesan, Otto Okun, Temitope Oloyede, Annamaria Pellegrino, Jacquie Pepall, Linda Peters, Anna Pritchard, Diana Prociv, Liyan Quan, Sowbhakya Rajabojan, Jessica Rizo Ricciardi, Sharmila Seetul, Adrian Sekretarczyk, Ranjita Sen, Lisa Shalet, Jeremy Silverstone, Anna Simpson, Roldan Singzon, Hettie Sizibo, Marie Subaran, Sarah Taylor, Victoria Todd, Annamaria Tommasi, Nerinne Truman, Stephanie Turton, Debora Twydell, Maryann Wairimu, Alexandra Ward, Paul Wilshaw, Tim Woolley, Summie Yeung. **Spring** Donald Adaakwah, Said Ahmed, Moteeb Akhtar, Saira Akhtar, Rahman Aklakur, Alvi Alam, Mahnoor Ali, Samad Ali, Michael Amankwa, Yunus Amin, Shae Andrew, Tilly Star Austin Walker, Mekdes Ayalew, Georgia Ayling, Abdul Azim, Bilkis Begum, Razmin Begum, Brieanna Bennett, Evie Binns, Omari Blackman, Emma Bradford, Sarah Broadway, Lisa Bunn, Jacob Butler, Thomas Caton, Lewis Chapman, Deborah Charman, Balraj Chatha, Anjum Choudhury, Labib Ahmed Choudhury, Amathul Chowdhry, Clive Christian, Naima Corbin, Hanna Cox, David Cullen, Lindsay Dale, Assunta De Biase, Franceline De Nazareth, Naomi Gegny, Terrie Duncan, Aaliyah Durant, Denise Durrell, Michael Fakkorede, Keeley Fletcher, Benjamin Frances, Joshua Fredericks, Alice Gaskell, Maureen Glynn, Mark Goodbody, Lea Grantham, Akilesultan Gullu, Imogen Hafford Tear, Ladonna Hall, Mia Hando, Gemma Hanmore, Alec Harris, Sarai Hayden, Jack Hearn, Noora Hossain, Margaret Hows, James Hucker, Amy Hughes, Maryam Javaid, Esha Javed, Max Jayatillake, Arti Katechia, Muhammad Khalid, Faheen Khan, Sazharul Khan, Umaima Khan, Jannatul Khijra, Christine Kinsella, Prince Kosoko, Megan Kyei, Debbie Le Flock, Summer-Jane Lewis, Daxa Maisuria, Dahni Maisuria, Janki Mankwana, Natalie Mann, Tasnim Maria, Megan Martyn, Kiran Matharu, Calvinder Mattoo, Douglas Mayther, Adem Mazreku, Shane Mccullough, Megan Mcintosh, Alison Melly, Kieron Melly, Reece Miles, Abbeyda Mohammed, Jill Moore, Isabelle Murray Pickard, Khanum Nadera, Laavanya Namby, Laxsana Namby, Jo Napp, Jamie Naulls, John Naulls, Miah Nayeem, Claudia Nguyen, Michelle Nguyen, Lewis Nimmick, Fiona Oakley, Lasairiona O'Baroid, Vicky O'Brien, Rayleigh O'Callaghan, Denise Oliver, David Olupitan, God'Smercy Oluwanusin, Muhammed Omarjee, Amar Panesar, Hanaa Pervez, Mark Pidduck, Subriya Qutubuddin, Aamina Rafi, Hafizur Rahman, Abdullah Bin Moklisur Rahman, Rabia Raza, Charlotte Reed, Tyler Reid, Robina Robinson, Jacob Rodriguez Quisberth, Benedict Sacarello, Asma Salim, Gulcin Sariyildiz, Michael Sayers, Lewis Scofield, Keiron Senyah, Tyshann Sewell, Shakila Siddiq, Arun Sivarajah, Oladapo Smith, Paul Soane, Grzegorz Sokolowski, Ned Sranadh Tanhai, Lucy Statham, Renae Steele, Jamie Stower, Tracey Sumner, Minhazzul Syed, Matthew Tayler, Brooke Taylor, Patricia Taylor, Christopher Thomas, Brooke Thompson, Ella Tobin, Charlee Tompkins, Wendy Tran, Jade Tuohy, Mohammed Uddin, Mohammad Uzair, Shanae Waite, Lois Ward, Jane Watson, Sarah Wilkinson, Davone Williams, June Willis, Madison-Ella Wilson O'Bong, Christine Wright, Tommy Covington Young. **Creative Team** Makayla Abraham, Ash Sohyun Ahn, Caroline Akselson, Jessica Albon, Tanya Alexander, Fatima Ali, Jahir Ali, Nazia Ali, Louise Allberry, Jennifer Allen, Justin Allin, Josephine Allitt, Shaimaa Alruwaished, Hana Amer, Katherine Anderson, Ashley Andrews, Maria Anning, Alicia Apaloo-Edwards, Jack Appleyard, Helene Arnesen, Isabella Asimadi, Storm Athill, Sophia Austen Meek, Sian Ayres, Yvonne Bailey, Mathura Balanadarasan, Sophie Bann, Claire Bannister, Rebecca Barclay, Penelope Bardoni, Lyndsey Barnewell, Matej Barszcz, Tonia Bastyan, Dean Batte, Natalie Beales, Daisy Beattie, Anna Beckett, Apia Begum, Shahania Begum, Shamama Begum, Katie Bell, Eki Belo-Osagie, Carol Belsten, Charlotte Bentham, Piotr Berkowicz, Agathe Bernardon, Deepti Bhalla, Sobia Bhatti, Grant Bigland, Jennifer Bigland, Gemma Bishop, Poppy Biswell, Chloe Blake, Matthew Blount, Kathleen Boland, Anna Bonomi, Natasha Bott, Charlotte Boulton, E Boussekson, Katie-May Boyd, Eve Bradshaw, Geno Brantley, Molly Bray, Eve Brayshaw, Bernadette Brennan, Eleanor Brereton, Amy Brian, Ross Britten, Olivia Broadbent Smith, Charlotte Brook, Gregory Brown, Claire Bunyard, Tazmin Burr, Lily Burrows, Eleanor Butcher, Lauren Butler, Sarah-Jane Caddock, Luman Cai, Fabianne Calitri, Grace Cameron, Charlotte Campbell, Stuart Campbell, Lisa Carracedo, Rachel Carter, Danielle Casey, Bridget Cass, Amy Cassell, Ella Chadwick, Bonnie Chai, Kit Shuen Chan, Yu Hui Chan, Ying Tung Chan, Rosie Chaplin, Nadine Chapman, Jason Charles, Grace Cheetham, Eponone Chen, Szu-Jung Chen, Viviane Chen, Xiaojing Chen, Dong Hoon Choi, Joanna Christou, Lidia Cimule, Loren Clark, Emma Connor, Victoria Conte, Alison Convery, Adam Cookson, Eleanor Coole-Green, Anne Cooper, Shaun Corcoran, Helga Cory-Wright, Florence Court, Chloe Cowan, Zac Coyle, Alex Crawford, Alexandra Cresswell, Amy Cresswell, Emma Cresswell, Connie Croasdale, Mary Cuffe, Danielle Cullen, Henrietta Curtis, Anna Czerniavska, David Daglish, Miriam Damanhuri, Alice Dan, Sharna David, Gabrielle Davies, Frances Davies, Holly Davies, Lucy Davis, Julia Day, Daniel Defreitas, Amy DeRees, Amanda Derrick, Joana Dias, Claire Docherty, Rebecca Doidge, Tatiana Dolmatovskaya, Blake Douglas, Harriet Dyson, Danielle Eagles, Anthony Earles, Harriette Earp, Samantha Easey, Joanna East, Carolyn Ebanks, Katie Eden, Bryony Edwards, Georgina Edwards, Maja Ehliar, Charlotte England, Gemma Evans, Constantina Evriviadou, Tobias

Volunteers

Fairclough, Josie Falconer, Aileen Faller, Jonathan Fensom, Sophie Finch, Wendy Foggin, Charley Fone, Edwin Ford, Rebecca Forknall, Luca Formica, Jessica Fournier D'Albe, Samantha Fox, Melissa Francis, Christabel Franklin, Chloe French, Marjorie Frick, Gemma Friel, Momoko Fujiwara, Katie Garden, Ruby Gaskell, Suchen Ge, Lauren Gee, Noella Geoghegan, Eleanor Gibson, Enka Gill, Caroline Gladwin, Beata Goaszweska, Joanna Goodman, Danielle Grant, Elizabeth Grant, Jessica Green, Elaine Guillon, Tharanga Gunawardena, Karen Gurney, Sandra Gustafsson, Zlatka Halkova, Melissa Hall, Jessica Halsey, Holly Hamblin, Kim Hamilton, Meng Hao, Alissa Harger, Iyo Hasegawa, Geraldine Hawkins, Alison Haworth, Jemma Haywood, Florence Hazard, Celestine Healy, Emma Heard, Audrey Elizabeth Hedgecock, Chloe Henderson, Holly Rose Henshaw, Clare Hepburn, Abigail Hernon, Francesca Hey, Amy Hickie, George Hims, Lysette Hodgson, Ruby Hodgson, Alix Holdaway-Salmon, Scarlett Hooper, Rachel Hopper, Sarah Hosein, Tina Hsu, Shuyi Huang, Chanel Huang, Jessica Hughes, Rosina Humphrey, Joanna Hunnisett, Toria Hunt, Jamila Hussain, Michelle Huynh, Silje Isaksen, Nur Ismail, Annan Jaggernauth, Gillian Jarvis, Rebecca Jempson, Laura Jenkins, Madeleine Jenkins, Katie Jenkinson, Laura Jenkinson, Charlotte Jepson, Amy Job, Bob Johnson, Margaret Johnson, Natasha Johnson, Georgia Jones, Lucy Jones, Rebecca Jones, Sophia Joseph, Eleanor Joyce, Holly Judd, Elizabeth Kane, Abul Kasam, Abul Kasam, Megan Keegan, Holly Keen, Tanya Keen, Muireann Kelly, Charlotte Kelly, Kristine Kenmochi, Ahhyun Kim, Joseph Kim-Suzuki, Harriet Kings, Leanne Kinnie, Osnat Koblenz, Veronika Kovacikova, Igli Kroqi, Georgina Lamb, Darren Lancett, Alexandra Langman, Sophie Langsford, Sara Laratro, Josie Lee, Tom Leggat, Demelza Leng, Caroline Lewis, Ge LI, Ruoxuan Li, Yangyang Li, Shuang Liang, Kate Lithgow, Roberta Lockett, Narash Lohia, Sue Lowe, Antonia Lynch, Emilie Lyons, Amy MacPherson, Emma Madray, Sara Maggi, Beverley Magtibay, Saad Mahmood, Rebecca Mahoney, Maria Mantilla, Ivan Manzella, Kathryn Marooney, Joanna Marshall, Anna Martin, Freya Martin, Sierra Martin, Tasha Marvell, John May, Ann-Marie Mays, Tansy McCluskie, Pete McDonagh, Jo McDonald, Sammi McGuigan, Michelle McHale, Letitia McLaughlin, Dorothy McLennan, Amy McPherson, Laura Meichtry, Olivia Catherine Mellowes, Cheramour Meoquanne, Florence Meredith, Gabrielle Milanese, Stephanie Miles, Jennifer Millen, Dan Miller, Darci Miller, Bo-Kyung Min, Clodagh Miskelly, Jasumati Mistry, Connor Mitchell, Hannah Mitchell, Sabrina Mohamed, Abigail Moller, Paula Gonzalez Montecino, Rosey Morling, Ronan Morrow, Madalaine Mould, Jillian Murray, Yuki Nakamura, Kamal Natt, Chloe Newman, Candice Newton, Billy Yu Lok Ng, Mandy Ngo, Fern Nolan, Jo Noon, Tanya Noor, Biannca Nugent, Michael Offei, Tosin Ogunsanya, Rebecca O'Higgins, Christina Omideyi, Zanna Orage, Zeanab Oshinbolu, Rainelle Osuji, Priscilla Otema, Lucy Packham-O'Brien, Sharon Page, Georgia Paget, Samuella Palmer, Natasha Payne, Donna Pendarvis, J. Childe Pendergast, Manavi Perera, Cathy Perkins, Fong Perry, Shamaela Perwiz, Louise Phelan, Gloria Enechojo Philip, Sabina Piccini, Hannah Pick, Andrew Pine, Patrick Pintaske, Lucy Pittard, Richard Pledge, Alice Pocock, Fiona Pollard, Claire Pompili, Lucy Ponting, Lara Prentice, Natasha Prynne, Faye Pulleyn, Anna Radecka, Syd Rae, Samantha Ranaweera, Kernisha Ransome, Nadia Rasheed, Harriet Reed, Megan Reidy, Natasha Ridley, Barbora Rimkova, Reenell Roach-Williams, Elizabeth Roberts, Mark Roberts, Pamela Roberts, Emma Robinson, Katherine Rogers, Madeleine Ross-Masson, Calista Ross-Peterson, Sophie Rowatt, Megan Rowlands, Sunita Sagoo, Nassima Saidani, Rachel Salenius, Clara Samuel, Kaylee Sanford, Billie Sanger, Marcio Santarosa, Pranav Sarin, Gerda Satunaite, Anna Saunders, Kate Seckington, Wamika Sehgal, Mai Seida, Rabeeah Shah, Melissa Sharpe, Sobia Shatti, Mengqin Shen, Deric Shen, Emma Sheppard, Poonam Shukla, Monika Sievers, Yana Simakova, Rachael Simpson, Gurfateh James Singh, Charlotte Slade, Charlotte Smith, Chris Smith, Lucia Smith, Mark Smith, Rosanna Smith, Emme Sparre-Slater, Angela Spink, Lorna Stimson, Camelia Sule, Kemi Sulola, Tamanna Sultana, Emma Sutcliffe, Philippa Sutcliffe, Hannah Sutherland, Sarah Sweet, Kazusa Takamura, Angel Tam, Nicola Tattersfield, Matthew Taylor, Molly Taylor, Poppy Taylor, Nicola Teale, Helena Tegeder, Marina Tegeder, Helen Thomas, PK Thummukgool, Kathryn Tickle, Mai Tieu, Beth Tilly, Charlie Todman, Bryony Tofton, Isabelle Tollitt, Billie Towers, Katherine Towerton, Julia Townend, Sekou Traore, Cecile Tremolieres, Louisa Trickett, Gina Trinchese, Anastasia Tsangarides, Melanie Tse, Alice Tucker, Beca Tuffnell, Jonathan Turner, Lisa Valde, Wendy Castano Vega, Sophie Venes, Ruby Vestey, Paul Vincent, Daniel Vincenze, Kalpani Vitharana, Tom Voller, Jana Vrabelova, Angela Wade, Caroline Walotka, Xiaoyun Wang, Victoria Watson, Jordan Watson, Elizabeth Webb, Jamey-Leigh Weber, Lianna Weidle, Jess Wheelband, Leanne White, Gianne Williams, Naomi Williams, Anna Witcombe, Finola Woolgar, Stephanie Woolven, Ying Wu, Lixiaoxue Xia, Jing Yang, Lanxiubo Yang, Yang Yang, Farhana Yeasmien, Amanda Yuan, Jovana Zarubica, Mona Zaw, Ruth Zewge, Xinyu Zhang, Yiyi Zhao, Min Zhou. **Technical Team** Tracy Abercombie, David Adkin, James Adkins, Mauricio Affonso, Ash Ahn, Christopher Amaning, Keren Amroussi, Eleanor Andrews, Nick Ashby, Theo Athanasopoulos, Miles Baldwin, Charlotte Banner, Jonathan Barlow, Andrea Bennett, Paul Bond, Nikki Boone, Becki Boot, Alastair Borland, Matt Boswood, Rachel Bottomley, Charlotte Boulton, Heather Bourne, Alex Braithwaite, Alex Bratza, Natalie Braune, Simon Brockwell, Chris Brown, Claudia Bryan-Joyce, Jess Buckley, Jarrett Bulat, Mike Burke, Rowan Burton, Elliot Carmichael, Becky Carolan, Kriss Carr, Laura Carus, Pamela Casasa, Danielle Casey, Claire Charlesworth, Tania Clarke, Peter Clerkin, Matthew Compton, Matt Compton, Itziar Coteron, Megan Courage, Lesley Covington, Roz Creusson, Reece Crisp, Moira Cross, Holly Curtis, Anna Czerniawska, Adam Dallman, Merlin Dass, Lee Davies, Christian Davies, Tom Davis, Amanda Derrick, Hannah Dimelow, Stuart Dingley, Ian Dixon-Wilkinson, Ben Donoghue, Grace Douetil, Myfanwy Dowding, Katie Ducarreaux, Alex Durrell, Sasja Ekenberg, Sandra Elsom, Susan Entwistle, Ilse Euser, Gabriella Fewster, Holly Fitch, Nathalie Fitzgerald, Luke Flint, Hazel Frame, Gemma French, Juno Frewing, Laizan Fung, Sean Gallacher, Jimmy Garner Currie, Jayne Gibson, Sam Gilham, Abi Gill, Lesley Gill, Caroline Gladwin, Phil Gomme, Adam Gray, Linda Gray, Erin Green, Simeon Green, Jamie Grossman, Charlie Hain, Laura Hammond, Kate Harries, Rachel Harris, Iain Harvey, Iyo Hasegawa, Joyce Hastings, Ceri Hazelden, Anthony Holme, Abby Holmes, Chris Howard, Emily Howie, Emma Hughes, Rebecca Humphreys, Hilary Hunt, Amy Insole, Sarah Jackson, Rory Jakeman, Piran Jeffcock, Charlie Johnson, Lisa Juergensen, Maria Kalamara, Helena Kanoute, Jessica Kelley, Francesca Kelly, Marie Kristine Kenmochi, Reese Kirsh, Olivia Alice Knight, Eleftherios Kotsis, Katie Kozlowska, Kemey Lafond, Jennie Leach, Nigel Letheren, Charlotte Levy, Qiming Liu, Chris Lloyd, Tink Lloyd, Edward Locke, Daisy Long, Sam Mannis, Theodora Marlas, Elisabetta Massimi, Hannah McArdle, Jo McDonald, Danielle McNiven, Marta Micallef, Hannah Moore, Josh Moore, Joe Morgan, Rikhil Morjaria, Luke Morton, Luisa Mota, Valerie Munday, Sophie Naisbitt, William Newman, Anna Newton, Anh Hoang Nguyen, James Nicholson, Katy Nixon, Sam Ohlsson, Connaire Packeer, Christina Palaiologou, Amelia Palmer-Johnston, Hannah Pardon, Joe Park, Heather Passmore, Matthew Peers, Ryan Penny, Alex Peters, Philip Peters, Theresa Pine, Patrick Pintaske, Ellie Pitt, Gareth Prentice, Beth Price Williams, AlisonPrior, Will Purton, David Putman, Alex Randall, Joe Ratcliffe, Sonia Razi, Caroline Rechter, Greg Reekie, Yuan Ren, Daisy Rigley, Daniel Roach- Williams, Jonathan Roberts, Thomas Robinson, Tom Robson, Seth Rook Williams, Jack Ryan, Alison Rycroft, Venetia Samuel, Priti Shah, Caroline Sheard, Kathryn Shooter, Jeremy Silverstone, Elliot Sinclair, Sophie Skelton, George Smith, Ollie Smith, Damien Stanton, Hannah Stewart, Sharna Stockdale, Sam Stuart, David Tague, Sabina Tajbhai, Karl Taylor, Ann Taylor, Richard Thurlow, Charlie Todman, George Townsend, Dave Train, Michael Trasmundi, Lucy Vann, James Wakerell, Luke Wallace, Paul Walmsley, Caroline Walotka, Becca Walters, George Walters, Louisa Ward, Shirley Ann Waterhouse, Gina Watson, Amy Watts, Ben Watts, Jenny Webster, Jack Weir, Tara Wells, Laura Whitley, Amy Whittle, Paul Williams, Anthony Willis-Osborne, Liz Wimms, Jon Wing, Jonathan Wright, Ben Yager, Noemi Zajzon. **Operations Team** Temitope Adetunji, Tryvell Allen-Charles, James Angel, Nabeel Arshad, Becki Austin, Dandan Bai, Loudmar Bento Portilho, Chris Blackledge, Cormac Bonar, Reece Bourne, Mary Boyes, Jenna Brailey, Doyin Brown, Delphie Callender-Foster, Laura Cantegreil, Jody Chappell, Meng Chen, Tianran Chen, Cheng Cheng, Amy Christie, Lea Clark, Sue Clarke, Christal Clashing O'Reilly, Alexandra Clipa, Nicholas Columbo, Joshua Connolly, Scott Crowhurst, Andrew Davidson, Gemma Davis, Li Ding, Andrea Donigan, Efi Doron, Farid Dudha, Laurene Duret, Katy Earth, Rowanne Eeles, Toby Erskine Crum, Rhea Foy, Mary Furlong, Vanda Galazka, Rosie Gamble, Gus Garcia Lopez, Charmaine Nicole Griffith-McCann, Emma Gyasi, Julie Haggar, Hannah Hand, Emma Hannibal, Coretta Hart, Suchita Hathiramani, Philomena Hayward, Jay Heard, Sophie Heath, Sze Lok Ho, Barbara Hochrath, Danielle Holland, Shan Howes, Minghan Hu, Chen Huang, Jessica Ibeh, Susan Johansson, Akshata Kamath, Tijana Kasic, Ambrosia Kejing Zhu, Michelle Lacey, Holly Laws, Martina Lee, William Leung, Yee Row Liew, Mei Chern Lim, Henry Lin, Sasha-Louise Lopez, Richard Lorde, Mark Luggar, Laura Macrae, Rob Madeley, Tanisha Malkki, Peter Marley, Shayesteh Mazloumian, Rachel McDermott, Sharon McElhinney, Ambre McGee, Peter McGuinness, Alexander McKinven, Anikta Mehta, King Mensah, Saira Mirza, Kirsty Moss, Hollie Munford, Carol Nascimento, Laura Nastase, Selena Ng, Sian Nicholas, Laura Oakley, Sarah-Jane O'Brien, Dawn O'Brien, Sevda Onder, Luis Ortega Contreras, Hilary Osei-Asibey, Julia Ouzia, Jonny Paim, Viktorija Panfilova, Wai Yee Pang, Louise A Panteli, Franklin Pate, Vaneshaben Patel, Kathy Peacock, Amanda Peck, Zoe Pickburn, Olivia Pole-Evans, Alexandra Redpath, Elizabeth Redpath, Tammy Rennie, Tim Reynolds, Olivia Roach, Niel Robbins, Joanna Rockliff, Sue Rowland, Jack Rule, Lena Ruprai, Nathan Ryan, Kimberley Sayers, Shreeya Shah, Mark Shannon, Bing Sheahan, Matilde Silva, Bhupinder Jit Singh, Aga Spiewak, James Stock, Yuka Tanaka, Kath Tatlock, Jack Tattersall, Alex Taylor, Carol-Ann Tennant, Ruth Tesfai, Emma Thompstone, Jeff Tong, Vuong Tong, Kate Tucker, Edson Sydney Tucker, Andrew van Blommestein, Nancy Vigrass, Benjamin Walker, Gavin Walsh, Charlie Welch, Toni Wong, Jing Zhao, Ji Zhu.
Thank you to the following group who appeared in the Ceremony Help for Heroes Band of Brothers **Thank you to the east London Host Borough schools whose pupils appeared in the Ceremony** Barking Abbey School, John Roan Secondary, Morpeth School, Woodside Primary **Thank you to all the Games-time role volunteers who contributed to the delivery of the Ceremony. And thank you to all the drama, dance, music and sports groups, societies, centres, organisations and clubs throughout the UK for all their help and support and for publicising our call for volunteers. We couldn't have done it without you.**

Delivering a memorable Paralympic Games to inspire a generation with the support of our Partners

Worldwide Paralympic Partners

London 2012 Paralympic Partners

      Sainsbury's

London 2012 Paralympic Supporters

London 2012 Paralympic Suppliers and Providers

Aggreko, Airwave, Atkins, The Boston Consulting Group, CBS Outdoor, Crystal CG, Eurostar, Freshfields Bruckhaus Deringer LLP, G4S, GlaxoSmithKline, Gymnova, Heathrow Airport, Heineken UK, Holiday Inn, John Lewis, McCann Worldgroup, Mondo, NATURE VALLEY, Next, Nielsen, Otto Bock, Populous, Rapiscan Systems, Rio Tinto, Technogym, Thames Water, Ticketmaster, Trebor, Westfield.